Change-Agent Skills B:
Managing Innovation and Change

Change-Agent Skills B:
Managing Innovation and Change

Gerard Egan, Ph.D.

Pfeiffer
& COMPANY

San Diego • Toronto
Amsterdam • Sydney

Copyright © 1988 by University Associates, Inc.

ISBN: 0-88390-220-6

Library of Congress Catalog Card Number: 88-10652

Printed in the United States of America

Library of Congress Cataloging-in-Publication Data

Egan, Gerard.
    Change-agent skills B.

    Companion to: Change-agent skills A: assessing and designing excellence.
    Bibliography: p.
    Includes index.
    1. Organizational change.   I. Egan, Gerard.
Change-agent skills A.   II. Title.
HD58.8.E37   1988   658.4'06   88-10652
ISBN 0-88390-220-6

Managing Editor: Mary Kitzmiller
Jacket Designer: Janet F. Colby
Production Artists: Janet F. Colby and William Bellomy

Preface

Change is the order of the day: either choose it or chase it. "Adapt or die" is the tag line that covers almost every business and organization. If there ever was a time when business-as-usual described the way businesses ran, that time has elapsed. Business-as-usual is today's prescription for going out of business. No one is immune to the forces of change.

Global competition. Technological change. The renewed value of human capital. Demographic changes that presage market shifts. The changing role and responsibility of governments. Corporate values. These crosscurrents challenge old assumptions and old practices. Not that everything tried and true should be abandoned; sometimes back-to-basics is the wave of the future. But the company that isn't actively re-examining its thinking is probably already dead from the neck up—and look out below! Companies on the move recognize that change begins as soon as you begin to think about how you think about what you do. Habits of mind govern habits of behavior. And a manager's mind is a terrible thing to waste.

> Alan M. Webber
> Managing Editor of the *Harvard Business Review*[1]

I often ask the people who manage the corporations, businesses, institutions, and agencies for which I provide consultancy services, the following question: "Would it be useful to have a relatively simple and straightforward shared model, framework, or template for business and organizational change?" They inevitably answer yes. However, when I put them to work to come up with the framework that they think is already in place or with one that would be useful

[1]Reprinted by permission of the *Harvard Business Review*. "In This Issue," by Alan M. Webber, Managing Editor (January-February 1988), p. 4. Copyright © 1988 by the President and Fellows of Harvard College; all rights reserved.

were it in place, the product they come up with, though usually better than their design-facilitation-assessment model (see the preface of *Change-Agent Skills A*, the companion to this volume), leaves much to be desired. I strongly believe that having such a common framework would help increase the productivity of most systems.

In books dealing with issues as complex as business and organizational change, there is inevitably a tradeoff between scholarly completeness and managerial usefulness. Indeed, if every item in the scholarly approach to change were to be attended to, planned change would never take place. In organizations there is a continuum of change from simple to complex. In the use of models of change there is also a continuum that goes from the use of the bare bones or even bits and pieces of a model to full use of all its stages and steps. This book provides an entire framework for change, but it has also proved useful in its bits and pieces.

This primer on making change happen is meant to provide hope for those who have tried system change and failed and for those wary of initiating change lest they fail. It is also meant to be a further incentive for those who have been successful. While the problems of change are in no way discounted, examples have been chosen to illustrate success, often success in the face of overwhelming odds.

Gerard Egan

Loyola University of Chicago
March 1, 1988

Contents

Introduction

In a higher world it is otherwise,
but here below to live is to change,
and to be perfect is to have changed often.

John Henry Cardinal Newman

In times of economic, social, and politial turbulence—and which era of human history has been without these?—the ability of a system to renew itself is critical. Leadership, whether at an executive, managerial, supervisory, or professional/technical level, is about managing innovation and change. Just as all the members of a system need to participate in the leadership *process*, so all—each in his or her own way—need to be "change masters" (Kanter, 1983):

> All people. On all fronts. In the finance department, the purchasing department, in the secretarial pool as well as the R&D group. People at all levels, including ordinary people at the grass roots and middle managers at the heads of departments, can contribute to solving organizational problems, to inventing new methods or pieces of strategy.
>
> These "corporate entrepreneurs" can help their organizations to experiment on unchartered territories and to move beyond what is known into the realm of innovation—if the power to do this is available, and if the organization knows how to take advantage of their enterprise. (p. 23)

One source of power is an understanding of and an ability to use a simple but effective model of innovation and change. The model for innovation and change that is the centerpiece of this book can be communicated to and used by everyone in a company, institution, and agency, enabling them to participate in the leadership process that characterizes institutions of excellence.

BEYOND STAGNATION
TO CREATIVITY AND INNOVATION

Too many companies, institutions, and agencies fail to create the kind of climate of vigilance and innovation that enable them to renew themselves even in the face of environmental turbulence. There is a wonderful passage from a recent novel called *The Finishing School* by Gail Godwin (1985). An older woman, Ursula, becomes a kind of mentor to a younger woman, named Justin. In this passage she is giving Justin a bit of her own brand of wisdom:

> "There are two kinds of people," she once decreed to me emphatically. "One kind, you can just tell by looking at them at what point they congealed into the final selves. It might be a very *nice* self, but you know that you can expect no more surprises from it. Whereas, the other kind keep moving, changing. . .They are *fluid*. They keep moving forward and making new trysts with life, and the motion of it keeps them young."

We all know organizations that have "congealed into their final selves." They might still be useful selves, but they offer little interest or excitement to those who come in contact with them and little challenge to those who work in them. Their continued survival in the face of turbulent environments is open to question. If change is nothing more than problem management, change agents can soon become disspirited. Worse, it supports the practice of seeing leadership as crisis management. Problems and crises are better seen in an upbeat fashion as challenges and opportunities.

> EXAMPLE: A crisis faced the Los Angeles County Public Administrator's Office in 1979. Budget reductions meant a 10 percent cut in staff, but the office was expected to maintain the same level of service to two thousand disabled people unable to care for themselves. In caring for the needs of these people, the office was responsible for the administration of ten thousand estates with total assets exceeding $150 million in cash, real estate, and personal property. The crisis was seen as a challenge: not just to maintain but to increase productivity despite the loss of twenty employees. The office used the crisis as an opportunity to automate many of its functions. A complete computer-based management information system (MIS) was installed, including

a case-management function that allowed the tracking of cases from start to finish. Forms usage, document inputs, and processing duplication were all significantly reduced. For instance, input documents were reduced from 1,002,360 to 83,530. The successful installation and implementation of the MIS system won an achievement award from the National Association of Counties in 1985. (See Los Angeles County Public Administrator, 1986.)

The problem with opportunities is that they often come disguised as risks. Accepting a challenge means accepting and working with the risks inherent in the challenge.

REASONABLE RISK TAKING

Organizations and institutions that get ahead often take risks, at least reasonable risks (Wriston, 1986), if this is not a contradiction in terms. This takes managerial courage. Hornstein (1986) recalls an executive's response to a needs analysis survey:

> "Beginning right now, organization success and survival will depend on challenging what we've been doing, on confronting existing organizational strategies, practices, and policy. It will require us to make certain that . . . key managers act courageously, telling us what's wrong, and not cower in organizational corners, vainly hoping that necessary changes will magically occur without their involvement." (p. 188)

Risk taking is a relative thing. For instance, Avemco is a leader in general aviation insurance. Its current chief executive officer (CEO) describes his approach to business as cautious. Avemco avoids insuring commercial, commuter, and unusual planes, nor does it handle million-dollar liability policies—except at stiff premiums. Avemco writes no more than 4 percent of its policies on business jets. Its CEO says that Avemco takes risks but makes sure the rewards are greater than the risks (Fix, 1986). In this case adopting a cautious strategy has paid off.

On the other hand, Wriston (1986) takes the business press to task for admonishing companies when they adopt "risky strategies." He says that there is no accomplishment without risk and that if managers do not take risks, they should be thrown out of their offices. In sum, there is a middle ground between change strategies that are reasonably risky and those that are merely foolhardy.

A MODEL FOR BUSINESS, GOVERNMENT, CHURCH, EDUCATION, AND HUMAN-SERVICE SYSTEMS

The model outlined in these pages, like Model A (Egan, 1988) applies to all sorts of systems. There is a tendency for each system to see itself as unique. There is something good in this. Each system, like each human being, needs a sense of identity, a "we are" feeling. However, a sense of identity or uniqueness is a two-edged sword. It can become a source of endless excuses: "Those models and methodologies might be fine for others, but not for us, because we are unique" is the cry of a system doomed to mediocrity, turmoil, or extinction. As in *Change-Agent Skills A* (a companion volume to this book), a large international airline, which we will refer to as "United International Airways" (a competitor of ABC Airways) will be used to illustrate the stages and steps of innovation and change. While the airline is fictitious, the examples are drawn from cases involving real airlines.

2

Overview of a Practical Model of Organizational Change

Model B, in its broadest outline, looks deceptively simple. It has three stages:

I. The Assessment of the Current Scenario.

II. The Creation of a Preferred Scenario.

III. Designing a Plan that Moves the System from the Current to the Preferred Scenario.

Since these three stages are essentially cognitive in nature, their ultimate justification is *action* that produces *valued outcomes or results* for the company or institution. Too many organizations expend a great deal of effort on change that leads nowhere. These three stages and their relationship to action or implementation are pictured graphically in Figure 2-1. Notice that the focal point of the model is action leading to desired outcomes. Planning for change is important, but only if it leads to valued, organization-enhancing outcomes.

I. *Current Scenario.* **Find out what's not going right or what's going wrong in terms of problems, unmet needs, unused resources, unexploited opportunities, unmet challenges, and so forth.**

> EXAMPLE: A California software company that created excellent financial-management packages for a variety of industries went out of business because it failed to manage its own finances well. Success and growth came quickly, too quickly. The founders and the special group that surrounded them knew a great deal about designing creative software and entrepreneurship but little about effective organizational controls. Of course, to the founders the very word "control" smacked of the Old whereas they were interested in the New. One example of

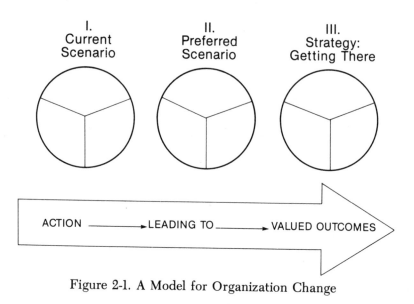

Figure 2-1. A Model for Organization Change

failed control deals with an interesting approach to "flex" time. Creative people, doing their own thing, worked long hours, banked their excess hours, and then disappeared for days and even weeks on end. Even when consultants were called in to help, they found it almost impossible to get the full story. Appointments with the two top people in the organization, who were by now at odds with each other, were canceled without notice. The whole dismal tale about an almost complete lack of essential controls began to leak out only at the end, when it was already too late.

A full organizational assessment spells out in detail both deficits in the current functioning of the system and unused opportunities. It answers the question: Why are we thinking of changing in the first place? Sometimes the mere identification of problems or opportunities is enough to galvanize an organization into action.

II. *Preferred Scenario.* Determine what the organization, organizational unit, program, or project would look like if it were in better shape. A preferred scenario deals with what an organization needs and wants, not with how it is to be achieved.

EXAMPLE: The management-development team of a mid-size East Coast organization, when asked, "What would your unit look like if it were functioning the way you would like it to function?" came up with answers such as the following:

- Tasks would be divided up more equitably. Too many of the creative tasks keep going to the same people.
- We would have enough slack time to keep up with the latest developments in our field. We would be reading the best books and taking seminars at the best management-development centers.
- Outside consultants now deliver many of our programs. We would deliver most programs; outside consultants would help us prepare to deliver them.
- We would have more time for follow up with clients. This would open the possibility of becoming consultants in the various departments.
- We would not be as rushed. We would design and redesign programs to avoid the last minute rushes that are killing us right now.

Note that these are all possibilities, which, when taken together, would constitute the full preferred scenario. Stage II deals with the search for and choice of outcomes, but this is meaningless if outcome-achieving action does not take place.

III. *Plan for Getting There.* **Develop an action program or strategy for moving the current scenario to the preferred scenario. Stage III deals with how results are to be accomplished.**

EXAMPLE: An automobile manufacturer decided that the company needed a trimmer organization. In less competitive times it was easy to reward people through promotion. But now, in much more competitive times, there were just too many layers of middle managers. A trimmer middle—the elimination of three layers of management and 35 percent fewer middle managers within two years—is what the organization wanted. The planners adopted a variety of strategies for achieving this outcome. First of all, they communicated to all managers the new organizational design that was to be in place in two years. They made it explicit to all in the organization that reward through promotion was a much less likely event. Attrition, therefore, was the first strategy. Then they mounted an aggressive early-retirement program. Those who decided that there was no future for themselves in the company were helped through outplacement programs. Some managers were offered a choice between demotion and leaving. At the end of the first year, managers who were not producing at the levels called for in their performance plans were let go.

This is, of course, the briefest of outlines of what a viable strategy for trimming an organization might look like.

At any point in this three-stage process it may become clear how an organization needs to act in order to produce system-enhancing outcomes. In that case, *action* in conjunction with further planning and reflection is called for.

Each of these three stages, as will be seen, has three subdivisions or steps. While the stages and steps are treated in a logical sequence in this overview, they do not necessarily happen in this logical order in actual cases. Rather the model is the background framework against which the actual change project is carried out. In any given change project each of these steps might not be developed formally. For instance, once a problem or unused opportunity is seen clearly, action leading to some valued outcome might take place immediately.

3

Action at the
Service of Outcomes

Peters and Waterman (1982) suggest that one of the characteristics of excellent companies is a bias for action. They also state:

> Big companies seem to foster huge laboratory operations that produce papers and patents by the ton, but rarely new products. These companies are besieged by vast interlocking sets of committees and task forces that drive out creativity and block action. (p. 120)

Smaller organizations and institutions, too, are quite inventive in finding ways to block action. On the other hand, productive organizations act and take reasonable risks in doing so. Again from Peters and Waterman (1982):

> The most important and visible outcropping of the action bias in the excellent companies is their willingness to try things out, to experiment. . . . There is no more important trait among the excellent companies than an action orientation. (pp. 134, 154)

The best organizations have a climate or culture of learning and problem solving. They know that there is no learning without experience and there is no experience without action. Figure 3-1 indicates how the stages of Model B are meant to drive action.

The management of change is not primarily about planning or action. It is about organization-enhancing outcomes. It is about results—innovations realized, problems managed, opportunities developed, new organization- and business-enhancing patterns of behavior in place. A large Midwest bank that had gone through disastrous times put the same advertisement in a number of different newspapers and magazines. The ad, a two-page spread, consisted

9

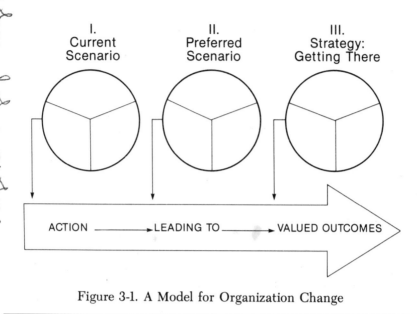

Figure 3-1. A Model for Organization Change

of the word "work" repeated over 100 times across the two pages. Below this were the words "A list of 1986 objectives." I would have felt more comfortable had the ad listed the word "outcomes" or "accomplishments" over 100 times. It was misguided action leading to disastrous outcomes that got the bank in trouble in the first place. The management of change is about planning and action only insofar as these lead efficiently and effectively to valued outcomes.

Since Stages I, II, and III—together with the steps within them—are important insofar as they are triggers and channels of action and since action can follow any step of Model B, it makes sense to explore action first. Action, usually under the rubric of program implementation, is considered last in most models of change. Perhaps that is why many attempts at organizational change "lose the name of action." The *doing* part is so far down the road that the change effort runs out of gas before getting there. Outcome-producing action is what makes the planning part of the model dynamic. Each of the three stages and nine steps must have action in its guts.

Planning is both essential and dangerous. If the organization does not plan well, change efforts can go off half-cocked. "Let's try this and see what happens" is not bad as a condiment but should not be a staple. On the other hand, Weick (1969) counsels against overplanning:

The point is simply that planning can insulate members from the very environment which they are trying to cope with. Planning in the absence of action is basically unconstrained; the only actions available for reflective attention are the planning acts themselves. The members can learn more and more about how to plan and how they are planning, but they can lose sight of what they were originally planning for. (p. 103)

What is called for often in organization change is a dialog between planning and action. Action is brash; it usually does not wait for the end of the planning process.

The model presented in these pages does not suggest postponing action until the perfect plan for change is in place. Weick (1979) goes so far as to suggest that "chaotic action is preferable to orderly inaction":

Action, when viewed retrospectively, clarifies what the organization is doing, what business it is in, and what its projects may be. Inaction, viewed retrospectively, is more puzzling and more senseless: there is a greater likelihood for bizarre meanings to be attached and for an unhealthy amount of autism to be introduced. Action, in other words, provides tangible items that can be attended to. . . . Thus, when there is confusion and some member of a group asks," What should I do?"and some other member says, "I don't know, just do something," that's probably a much better piece of advice than you might realize. (pp. 245-246)

Weick adds that this is better advice because it increases the likelihood that something will be generated that can be made meaningful. Weick does not suggest that chaotic activity is best, but it is certainly better than endless planning and talk about change that promise much and deliver little.

I attended a meeting of a personnel department task force enjoined with the development of a performance planning and appraisal system. I had been asked to observe and comment on the meeting. The man in charge, standing before a phalanx of flip charts, started by pointing to the charts and saying, "These are the twenty-four tasks that remain to be accomplished before we can start implementing the system." I was dumbfounded, because they had already been at work for almost a year. When asked to comment at the end of the meeting, I said something like this: "Performance planning and appraisal are, in concept at least, basically simple. Therefore, I've been asking myself why it's being made so complicated. I see at least two reasons. First, there is a culture of perfectionism in this organization that runs riot most of the time. Second, many of the comments made at this meeting suggest that you expect massive resistance from managers. You are trying to manage the expected resistance by coming up with the perfect plan. Both of these keep you in the relatively safe harbor of planning. My bet is that action at this point is seen as too dangerous. But I also believe that it is time to *do* something." This is not to say that planning for change is not essential. Planning engaged in by people who have a healthy skepticism about its efficacy can be very productive.

One of the first things that John Egan did when he was made CEO of the then languishing Jaguar was to visit the factory in Coventry. It was a mess. He ordered that it be immediately cleaned and painted, then had American dealers over for a tour. This hardly took care of all of Jaguar's problems, but it did send a signal to everyone that things were going to be different at Jaguar.

EXAMPLE: The new director of human resources at United International Airways inherited a department plagued with problems. Most of the line managers considered the department a bloated bureaucracy that caused rather then solved problems. Getting around personnel policies and procedures was one of their favorite games.

The director, after briefly reviewing a number of renewal strategies, decided to use the performance planning and appraisal system as the vehicle of change. He called in his top managers, explained the new service mission of the human resources department, had each of them read *Service America* (Albrecht & Zemke, 1985), reviewed the sad list of complaints about the services of their units, gave them each three weeks to draw up new, tough performance objectives (both unit and individual), told them to do the same for everyone that reported to them, and then asked them to come up with a list of actions that could be taken *immediately* in order to improve the performance of their units.

The best predictor of the ultimate outcomes of change efforts is the action that does or does not take place between the first and the second planning meetings. If people leave the first meeting and do nothing before the second meeting, this sets the tone for the change project—"It's not about doing, it's about talking." The president of a small college noticed that his executive team made many decisions but implemented few of them. At the advice of a consultant, the regular minutes were replaced by "action minutes." That is, each meeting ended with decisions about actions that needed to be taken. The first part of the next meeting was spent reporting on the status of these actions.

underpining of culture

MANAGING RESISTANCE: THE PERVASIVENESS OF INERTIA AND ENTROPY

The three certain things in life are death, taxes, and resistance to change. The resisters have it easy. They can sit back and merely let two of the most powerful forces of nature—inertia and entropy—take over. Only if the system is dead serious about change do the resisters have to *do* anything to prevent change. Even then the odds are on the side of the resisters. Covert forms of sabotage are legion.

Inertia. Most change efforts fail because they are never really tried. A consultant mounted a large-scale action-research change project at a large corporation. The assessment work was done, change plans drawn up, and responsibilities assigned. He returned six months later to see how things were going. Nothing had been done. Inertia aided and abetted by the day-to-day running of the corporation had won out. Wise change agents, whether consultants, managers, or others, accept inertia as a fact of organizational life. It is not *whether* it will plague a change project but what *form* it will take. If action is an improbable event, then strategies need to be devised to ensure that it will take place. When the previously mentioned consultant returned, he had a number of conversations with the vice president of research and development and the vice president of manufacturing. The dialog went something like this:

Consultant: "Six months ago you said that you had some pressing issues to work out between your two departments, but you haven't got around to it."

VPs: "That's right."

C: "When are you going to meet?"

R&D: "We should get together soon."

C: "When are you going to meet?"

Mfgr: "We need to do so within the next month.

C: "When are you going to meet?"

R&D: "Maybe we could do it within the next two weeks."

C: "When are you going to meet?

Mfgr: "How about next week?"

C: "When are you going to meet?"

R&D: "How about next Tuesday?"

Mfgr: "I think that's OK."

C: "When are you going to meet?"

Mfgr: "How about 3:00?"

R&D: "Fine."

C: "*Where* are you going to meet?"

R&D: "Is my office all right?"

Mfgr: "Yeah."

The consultant went on to ask further questions, for instance, about the issues that would be discussed at the meeting. He did all of this to dramatize the overpowering nature of inertia and the need for commitment to specific actions to overcome it. Individuals and corporations alike are ingenious in inventing excuses, all of them noble, for not acting. It is in this context that Weick's preference for chaotic action over orderly inaction makes eminent sense. While vision is an important part of leadership (Bennis & Nanus, 1985), realistic *agendas* that flow from that vision are just as important. Creativity, if restricted to new *ideas*, is not enough. *Innovation* is creativity in action; innovation means making creative ideas work for humankind.

It is impossible to list all possible forms of resistance to innovation and change. However, it is possible to suggest a *framework* for dealing with every conceivable form of resistance. **That framework is Model B itself applied to whatever form of resistance arises.** It looks something like this:

- **The Current Scenario.** Identify the forms of resistance that block the way of the proposed project.

- **The Preferred Scenario.** Describe what it would be like if these forms of resistance were managed.

- **Strategies for Getting There.** Brainstorm a range of strategies for managing each form of resistance and set up an action plan for dealing with each.

Entropy, the tendency for human things to fall apart, is the second major plague of innovation and change. It will be considered in Chapter 16.

STAGE I

THE CURRENT SCENARIO

Overview

Assessing Problems and Opportunities

Challenging Blind Spots and
Developing New Perspectives

Leverage—the Search for High-Impact
Problems and Opportunities

4

An Overview of Stage I:
The Current Scenario

Stage I has three distinct but interrelated steps:

A. Assessing problems and opportunities.

B. Managing blind spots.

C. Choosing high-impact problems or opportunities for attention.

Below are brief overviews and illustrations of these three steps.

A. Assess deficits and identify unused opportunities. Companies and institutions with "cultures of vigilance" are constantly monitoring both emerging problems and opportunities. All companies and institutions have both problems and unused opportunities. The best get at the roots of chronic performance problems and missed opportunities and do something about them.

For instance, Hadley (1986) pinpoints six chronic problems that underlie the persistent snafus that seem to plague the United States defense establishment. First of all, he sees a vast social and cultural gulf between the military and the rest of American society. Until recently, most enlisted men came from limited economic and social segments of society. Second is what Kanter (1983) calls "segmentalism." In the military it takes the form of interservice rivalry leading to all sorts of blunders and inefficiencies. Third, the power of the chairman of the Joint Chiefs of Staff is eroded by politics. Management is by committees whose membership, by law, changes constantly. Fourth, there is no clear strategy for allocating resources between support functions and combat forces or between new hardware and maintenance. Fifth is the overcontrol from Washington. The wonders of modern electronics allow Washington to control the smallest operational details. In Iran, during the abortive mission to rescue the hostages, troops waiting in the desert for helicopters were barraged by messages from the White House but could not communicate with the helicopters because the radio frequencies did not mesh. Sixth is personnel mismanagement. The best people are assigned by the military services to missions most vital to their self-interest. Other areas, like procurement, become "pastures for the marginally competent." Hence, $700 toilet seats and $400 hammers.

On the other hand, it is just as important to keep looking for opportunities and better ways in which to use resources. This kind of creative vigilance is not the norm for either individuals or institutions. As Hickman and Silva (1984) state:

> Since none of us lives long enough to experience everything, we can easily be trapped within a rigid set of habits, underutilizing our experience and greatly reducing our ability to spot opportunities, create advantages, and devise solutions to problems. Multiple perspectives free us to maximize our experience. (p. 100)

Two entrepreneurs have created businesses out of identifying and developing opportunities. The following example is based on an article in *Business Week* ("John Psarouthakis," 1986):

> EXAMPLE: John Psarouthakis buys undervalued, underperforming manufacturers and whips them into shape. After buying a company, usually a producer of such staid products as toilet bowls or transmission bearings, he installs a management team, modernizes technology, and secures the cooperation of line workers in making the plant more efficient. This has made his company, JP industries, highly profitable. (p. 74)

The next example (from Leonard, 1986) shows that John (Jay) Jordan of the Jordan Company takes a somewhat different tack:

> EXAMPLE: Jordan scours the heartland of America for privately owned companies making mundane, but profitable products such as rope, lamps, and plumbing products. These companies are often owned by an aging entrepreneur who is reluctant to sell for fear of what might happen to employees. Jordan offers deals in which key employees are offered equity stakes up to 50 percent. He then sits down with management to plot expansion and the financing needed to do it. (p. 56)

The same process can be used within businesses and institutions. It entails monitoring both the organization and the business environment for unused resources and untapped opportunities.

B. Challenge blind spots and develop new perspectives. John Gardner is quoted by Hickman and Silva (1984, p. 273) as saying, "Most ailing organizations have developed a functional blindness to their own defects. They are not suffering because they cannot resolve their problems but because they cannot see their problems." Curtis Publishing Company, publisher of *Saturday Evening Post*, became blind to market trends that took shape in the late Forties and Fifties and went out of business. Examples of companies and institutions stumbling over their own blind spots are legion. The following example is based on Geneen & Moscow (1984):

> EXAMPLE: ITT, thinking that it had the know-how to do well in the hotel business, bought the Sheraton chain in 1968, at the time hardly the industry leader. Despite a whole range of problems—such as lack of expertise in building hotels, failure to get expected financing, and running for years in the red—ITT persisted. A number of remedies were tried (e.g., getting rid of Sheraton management and substituting ITT managers, trying to run Sheraton like a rent-a-car business, and letting financial geniuses loose on the Sheraton problems), but all failed. Finally, a seasoned hotel man took a different look at the problem. He said in effect: "We've been blind. We're good at management but poor at real estate." This new perspective led to an entirely new scenario: Sheraton got out of the brick-and-mortar part of the hotel business and into managing the hotels. This strategy proved highly effective.

Companies and institutions willing to admit that they develop blind spots and willing to do whatever is necessary to have them challenged are much more likely to pursue excellence than those that remain defensive about their shortcomings.

C. Choose high-impact problems and opportunities. The following example illustrates how a company or institution can search for high-leverage problems and opportunities and establish change priorities.

EXAMPLE: A small chemical firm, while conducting a thorough organizational review, found a variety of problems. No one was quite sure what the mission of the company was nor what business niche they were trying to carve out for themselves. The interactions between R&D and manufacturing, however infrequent, were hostile. Staffing procedures were poor and often centered around personality rather than competency. Little empires were beginning to crop up everywhere. There was no aggressive customer development program. Customer complaints, though relatively infrequent, were handled poorly. Little attention was being paid to the environment—competitors, changing markets, economic trends in the industry, and so forth. Turnover was high in some departments. A range of other problems surfaced, but none seemed life threatening. The company was wallowing.

The problem chosen for immediate attention was the lack of a clear mission together with a crisp but flexible business plan. Many of the other problems and unexploited opportunities were rooted in this lack of organization direction.

In the Defense Department example, interservice rivalry lies at the root of many snafus. It is, then, a high-priority problem.

A TEMPLATE FOR ASSESSMENT

It is extremely useful to have a model, framework, or template of business and organizational effectiveness in order to search out systematically both deficits and opportunities, to uncover blind spots, and to identify leverage points. Model A (see Egan, 1988, the companion to this book) is precisely such a template. Model A answers questions such as "How do we design effectiveness and excellence into the system?" and "How do we assure excellence in functioning?" While Model B deals with the pragmatics of organizational change and problem solving, Model A deals with the pragmatics of functional excellence. The following is an overview of Model A.

AN OVERVIEW OF MODEL A

Model A has four major parts: business dimensions, organizational dimensions, leadership, and managing the shadow side of the organization. Each part contains a number of elements.

I. Business Dimensions

The business dimensions of Model A focus on the establishment of markets and the delivery of quality products or services to clients or customers. There are both strategic and operational business dimensions.

Strategic Business Elements

The strategic business elements give direction and purpose to the company or institution. They include the following:

- **Markets, Customers, Clients.** Viable markets need to be identified; customer needs and wants within these markets need to be explored.

- **Business Environment.** The business environment—competition, economic and social trends, new markets, emerging technology—needs to be scanned frequently for threats and opportunities.

- **Mission.** A business mission or overall purpose needs to be developed together with a parallel and integrated *people* mission.

- **Business Philosophy.** An integrated set of values and policies needs to be formulated to govern the conduct of business.

- **Major Business Categories.** The major categories of products or services to be delivered to customers in selected markets need to be determined.

- **Basic Financing.** The system needs to be established on a solid financial foundation. Many enterprises, poorly capitalized, fail before they really get off the ground.

- **Strategic Plan.** All these elements need to be addressed and pulled together into a strategic plan that sets the longer-term direction and goals of the system.

Operational Business Elements

Operational business elements refer to the day-to-day business of the company or institution. They include the following:

- **Products/Services.** Specific high-quality products and/or services that meet the needs and wants of customers need to be designed, manufactured, marketed, and delivered.

- **Work Programs.** Step-by-step work programs that assure the efficient production and delivery of high-quality products and/or services need to be developed.

- **Material Resources.** Effective programs for choosing and using the material resources, including financial resources, to be used in work programs need to be established.

- **Unit Performance Plan.** Each unit has its own set of operations that contribute directly or indirectly to the delivery of products and services to customers. The unit performance plan sets year-long operational priorities for the unit and links operations to the overall strategy of the enterprise.

II. Organizational Dimensions

The organizational dimensions include the structure of the organization, that is, functional units and subunits, and the deployment and utilization of human resources within these units. They include the following:

- **Structure and the Division of Labor.** Functional work units need to be established. Within these units, roles with clear-cut job descriptions and responsibilities need to be set up.

- **Competence.** The units and the people working in the units *def.* must be competent, that is, capable of achieving business outcomes. Once jobs with clear-cut job descriptions are established, competent

cf. core competencies - to begin

and compatible people need to be hired into these jobs and effectively socialized into the culture of the organization.

• **Teamwork.** Processes need to be established to ensure that units and people within units work together in teams whenever working together will deliver better business outcomes.

• **Communication.** Since communication is the lifeblood of the system, the organizational culture must call for (and individuals must have the skills needed for) effective information sharing, feedback, appraisal, problem solving, innovation, and conflict management among both units and individuals in units.

• **Reward System.** Incentives to do all the above must be provided, disincentives must be controlled, and performance rather than nonperformance must be rewarded.

• **Individual Performance Plans.** A sense of strategy or direction must permeate the entire system. Individual performance plans, established through dialog between individuals and their supervisors, focus yearly work priorities for each person in the system. These plans link individual efforts to the unit performance plan and—through this plan—to the overall strategy of the system.

III. Management and Leadership

If all the above is to happen, companies, institutions, and agencies need both effective management and ongoing leadership.

Management

Effective managers coordinate and facilitate all the business and organizational elements of Model A. They make things happen; but they make things happen through others. As managers of people, they make sure workers know what is expected of them, create clear paths to goals, provide resources and support, give feedback, monitor progress, and reward performance.

Leadership

Leadership is an interactive *process* involving the leader, team members or associates, and changing situations. Leadership goes beyond mere management to innovation and change. Leadership can be found at all levels:

- Executive
- Managerial
- Supervisory
- Professional/Technical
- Operational

Effective leadership is not predicated on the *traits* of the leader but rather on what he or she actually *accomplishes*. Leadership means (a) developing visions, (b) turning visions into workable agendas, (c) communicating these agendas to others in a way that results in excitement about and commitment to them, (d) creating a climate and ferment of problem solving and learning around the agendas, and (e) making sure that everyone persists until the agendas are actually accomplished. Leadership, in this sense, is at the heart of the search for excellence.

IV. Managing the Shadow Side of the Organization

The topic of managing the shadow side is not covered in this book. The author plans to make it the subject of a separate book at a later date. Nevertheless, it is so important that it needs to be mentioned briefly at this point.

The shadow side of an organization includes the arational factors that affect both the business and organizational dimensions of the system. Wise managers know how to deal with the following elements:

- **The Natural Messiness of Organizations.** Organizations are loosely coupled systems in which the kinds of rationality outlined in Sections I, II, and III are only approximated. For instance, strategy and operations are not always well integrated.

• **Individual Differences.** Individuals working within systems have their differences, idiosyncrasies, and problems, all of which need to be addressed and managed. Research shows that people in leadership positions often imprint their traits, good or bad, on the organization.

• **The Organization as a Social System.** Organizations are social systems with all the benefits and drawbacks of such systems. Internal relationships and cliques develop that can help or hinder the business of the system.

• **The Organization as a Political System.** Because most organizations must deal with scarce resources and differences in ideology, they are political systems. Some people put self-interest ahead of the business agendas of the company or institution.

• **Organizational Culture.** Organizations tend to develop their own cultures and subcultures. The shared beliefs, values, and assumptions in an organization can either enhance or limit the system's effectiveness. The culture is the largest and most controlling of the systems, because it sets norms for what may or may not be done in all the other "shadow-side" areas.

The ability to manage the shadow side of the organization often makes the difference between a successful or unsuccessful manager or between a mediocre and an excellent manager.

Provisions of Model A

Model A is a business and organizational effectiveness model. It provides the following:

• An integrative framework for understanding companies, institutions, and their subunits.

- A template for designing and running a system.
- An instrument for assessing the effectiveness of a system and for choosing remedial interventions.
- A common language for talking about systems.
- A map for helping to understand the *geography* of systems and to make their way around in them.

It is against the background of Model A that system innovation and change will be considered. In the next three chapters each of the steps of Stage I will be described and illustrated.

5

Step I-A:
Assessing Problems
and Opportunities

This is the the first step in the assessment stage. The outcome sought in this step is a clear understanding of the problems and opportunities facing the company or institution. Figure 5-1 adds Step I-A to the first stage of the model. What is the current scenario and what in this scenario calls for change? The current scenario can be looked at from a point of view of a deficiency and/or an opportunity.

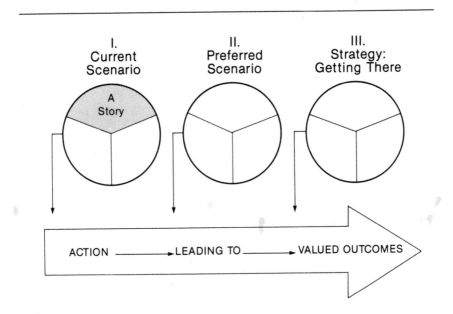

Figure 5-1. A Model for Organization Change

Deficiencies

[handwritten: asking strategy questions to lyr to culture]

The following questions can help to identify deficiencies:

- What crises are we currently facing?
- What is going wrong?
- What are our weaknesses, faults, and deficiencies?
- What are we failing to do well?
- In what ways are we falling short of what the best organizations in our field are doing?

Opportunities

The following questions can help to identify opportunities:

- What are our strengths, especially our unused strengths?
- What challenges do we need to respond to?
- What opportunities have we been ignoring?
- What overlooked markets should we explore?
- What innovative products or services might we offer?
- How can we improve the products or services we currently offer?
- In what ways could we be using our resources better?
- How strong is our will to become an exemplar in our field?

While both deficiency and opportunity approaches to assessing the current situation in the company, organizational unit, or project are useful and even essential, the model as used in these pages will stress the development of opportunities together with the leadership and imagination needed to do so. This means identifying opportunities that are buried in problem situations. For instance, the major oil companies, while suffering from a dramatic drop in oil prices, use turbulent times as an opportunity for buying reserves from smaller companies who have been hit harder and are struggling with cash flow problems. Opportunities and problems can appear in all the major dimensions of Model A—business, organizational, management, leadership, and shadow side.

TELLING THE ORGANIZATIONAL "STORY"

Step I-A deals with the search for unused opportunities and ignored or unmanaged problems. This means getting the organization to "tell its story." Like the stories of clients in counseling, the more honest and specific the story is, the more likely it will serve as the starting point for constructive problem management, innovation, and change. Organizations, like people, can engage in self-deception. As we saw in Chapter 2 in the example of the software company, the real story sometimes comes out only when the organization fails. United International Airways (UIA), using Model A as a template, does a thorough assessment of its business, organization, management, and leadership strengths and weaknesses.

EXAMPLE: UIA has a range of problems and unused opportunities. Some relate to the business. They have not developed a coherent post-deregulation strategy. For instance, a number of top managers believe that selective markets and creative agreements with other carriers are the wave of the future. Trying to cover the entire globe, they say, makes the airline too vulnerable, especially if deregulation, started in the United States, spreads to other countries.

Some managers are convinced that their airline has to get out of the transportation business and into the service business, meaning that UIA should see itself as a service business that happens to be in the transportation business. They see the people who are in direct contact with customers, both business and leisure travelers, as lacking both the skills and the authority needed to interact creatively with passengers. Its departure record is poor. And those who do fly UIA do so in spite of its catering service.

Some of UIA's problems are organizational or focus on management and leadership. There are too many layers of middle managers. Many of them have a pre-deregulation mentality. They do what they have to and do not want to be disturbed; a significant number of middle managers are marking time until retirement. Some of the better managers say, "We have a performance appraisal system, but it's merely a ritual, in many ways an organizational joke. For a variety of reasons, managers and supervisors either avoid writing the appraisals—80 percent are over six months late—or write perfunctory appraisals that help neither the company nor its employees." Other internal problems include the following: Too many top-level managers are without vision; career opportunities in terms of promotion have dried up; and because of recent layoffs, morale is low. Many of the departments of UIA are overstaffed and poorly coordinated; this is one of the reasons for the poor departure record. UIA has a poor history of labor relations, especially with its pilots. The trick is to find the opportunities that are buried in these problems.

On the other hand, UIA has a number of business strengths that constitute the bases for opportunities. It is in decent financial shape with comparatively little long-term debt. The fleet is aging but is in good mechanical repair. Given the number of cities it covers, there is the possibility of establishing one or two more strong hubs. UIA is also in a good position to establish mutually beneficial working relationships with a range of commuter airlines. Its excellent financial position provides opportunities for purchasing routes from other airlines and pushing into new international markets.

There are also a number of organizational and leadership strengths. Many people in UIA from top to bottom identify with the company and are eager to see it become one of the best airlines in the business. The new CEO has already won the respect of the people with whom he has met. And, although the history of the relationship between management and the unions has been a troubled one, there are indications that both management and unions are ready for a more creative relationship. The best and the brightest on both sides see that the future demands a partnership rather than an adversarial relationship.

This is merely a quick glance at some of the business and organizational problems and opportunities at UIA. Each organizational unit in the airline has its own set of problems and unused opportunities. However, it seems clear that now is the time for action at every level in the organization.

A CULTURE OF VIGILANCE

Janis and Mann (1977), in discussing problem solving and decision making, contrast vigilance with complacency. The best companies and institutions develop "cultures of vigilance." This includes:

• **Problem prevention.** The company or institution does not wait for problems to happen. Problem prevention is just as important as problem solving. Questions such as "How can this project go wrong?"

are not signs of despair, because they are immediately followed by "And what do we need to do to make sure that it doesn't go wrong?" Such enterprises are not habitually taken by surprise.

• **Problem Finding.** Problems are closely associated with opportunities, so that problem finding is associated with creativity. Bennis and Nanus (1985) state:[1]

> A creative mental process occurs when neither the problem nor the method, let alone the solution, exists as a known entity. Creativity involves a "discovered problem," one that needs to be worked out from the beginning to the end. The highest form of discovery always requires problem finding. This is very like the identification of a new direction or vision for an organization. (p. 41)

In the old UIA people were punished, often subtly, for pointing out problems. They were treated like whistle blowers. In the new, the reward system needs to be changed to encourage not only problem finding but also identifying the opportunities hidden in problems.

• **Opportunity Identification.** The best companies and institutions are always looking for opportunities. For instance, Robert Shulman, the CEO of Bolar, a small pharmaceutical company, took immediate advantage of the Waxman bill—which sharply reduced costs of gaining FDA approval for making generic equivalents of brand-name drugs. The day after the bill became effective, he submitted several dozen binders of generic-drug applications in person to the FDA office in Washington. Identification of and response to opportunity, which Shulman calls "mobility of management," combined with marketing savvy, have made Bolar a profitable company (see Merwin, 1987). A culture of vigilance means much more than spying the wolf at the door, that is, looking for problems to solve, looking for mediocrity so it can be rooted out, and looking for threats to manage. It means developing an eye for opportunities even in the midst of adversity. Opportunities seldom knock loudly. Vigilance, as used here, is not meant to be just a set of practices; it needs to become

---

[1]From *Leaders: The Strategies for Taking Charge* (p. 41) by W. Bennis and B. Nanus, 1985, New York: Harper & Row. Reprinted with permission.

a part of the culture of the system. It is not easy to establish a culture of problem-finding and opportunity-identifying vigilance. In most organizations the prevailing culture is most likely to be one that supports ignoring problems until they turn into crises. This promotes a culture of crisis management.

MODEL A AS A VIGILANCE GRID

Model A (Egan, 1988), which is summarized in Chapter 4, and the questions (see Appendix A) it asks about each element of the model, provide the framework for establishing a culture of vigilance, an ongoing systematic scan of both internal and external environments for emerging problems and opportunities. Figure 5-2 turns Model A into a "vigilance grid." Questions on each element of the model have been designed to provide data about business, organizational, management, and leadership factors. Companies and institutions with cultures of vigilance know how to collect and analyze hard data at the service of change programs. Regular meetings and brainstorming sessions are held throughout the organization in search of emerging problems and opportunities.

	PROBLEMS	OPPORTUNITIES
Business		
Organization		
Management		
Leadership		
The Culture		

These are the major categories of Model A. The questions for each element within these categories (see Appendix A) constitute a total system scan. The grid can be used in all organizational processes through which problems, deficits, and opportunities are identified: routine and special data collection and measurement processes, regular staff meetings, regular managerial reviews, formal and informal data-producing interactions with clients or customers, brainstorming sessions, and cross-level listening sessions, task-force meetings, and so forth.

Figure 5-2. The Vigilance Grid

United International Airways wants to move toward a culture of vigilance. Here are some of the things they are doing in business areas.

• **Scanning the Business Environment.** The business environment is routinely and systematically scanned for emerging problems and opportunities.

EXAMPLE: UIA realizes that a culture of vigilance is absolutely necessary in the turbulent airline industry. It is especially critical to monitor changes in the economic environment, especially economic slumps and recessions. However, it has been demonstrated that slumps are usually well under way before they are spotted (see *Business Week,* January 12, 1987, p. 32). The financial unit at UIA sets about developing more timely slump and recession indicators. Speed in adapting to business slumps can give UIA an edge over its competitors.

Hard data and intuition need to be combined to provide information on which innovation and change decisions can be based.

• **Discovering Problems/Opportunities Through Interactions with Customers.** The automotive industry did not know that it was in trouble with its customers until massive inroads in the marketplace by foreign carmakers made it crystal clear. There are a number of ways of gathering the kind of information from clients that can stimulate change:

1. Informal discussions with clients about their needs and their satisfactions or dissatisfactions with the products or services supplied to them.

2. Formal customer or client surveys.

3. Careful review of customer complaints with a view to identifying patterns related to the quality and value of products or services and also the quality of customer service.

EXAMPLE: The automotive industry has never had a history of responding well to customer complaints. UIA believes that the airline industry cannot make the same mistakes. On the contrary, customer complaints must be seen as sources of important information. For instance, there are many complaints about catering. Some at UIA say that passengers choose an airline because of convenience of schedules and discounted fares and not because of food. However, others argue that providing mediocre meals means that the customer-service strategy is a lie. Poor food becomes a symbol of how the airline really feels about its passengers. The director of catering is replaced and it is soon apparent that good meals are more a question of imagination than money. Food variety and quality goes up while costs remain about the same.

Workers can be encouraged to solicit feedback from customers; the data collected form an early-warning system. However, those in direct contact with customers need to be trained to listen carefully without defending themselves or the company too quickly. They need to take complaints seriously and be open to suggestions, especially from unexpected sources.

Similar methodologies can be used to review the remaining business elements of Model A together with organizational, management, leadership, and shadow-side dimensions. Companies and institutions with cultures of vigilance cut across the organization in efforts to identify both problems and opportunities. Cross-level listening sessions are opportunities for staff members across two or more levels to discuss their work as they see it. Managers simply listen for issues, problems, and opportunities.

PERSISTENT PROBLEMS
AND ORGANIZATION CULTURE

Many organizations have problems that seem intractable. Everyone knows that they exist, but no one seems to be able to do anything about them. For instance, everyone in a large development bank knew that there were too many people checking the same reports, but, even though everyone complained about it, the problem persisted. Why was the problem so difficult to manage? In a word, because of the *culture* of the organization. It was an organization filled with top professionals that over the years had created a culture, not just of professionalism, but of perfectionism. Everything had to be perfect. Process took precedence over outcome. Even relatively trivial documents had to be perfect. The institution was less efficient than it might be because it wasted its resources in the pursuit, not just of valued outcomes, but of perfection.

> EXAMPLE: Everyone at UIA knew that the organization produced too much paper. There were too many reports, too many memos. In fact, the written word was used routinely when the spoken word would have been much more effective. For instance, managers, instead of giving feedback informally, would send memos to their workers. Employees jokingly called these memos "snowflakes." Again, everyone at UIA knew that there was too much paper, but no one seemed to be able to do anything about it. Even when senior managers *decreed* that there would be less paper, little happened.

There is often an organization-culture dimension to problems when:

- People in the organization are aware of and talk about them.
- They are chronic rather than new.
- They have resisted change over a period of time.
- They are widespread.
- There is a sense of fatalism about them.

These conditions certainly characterize the UIA paper problem.

Organization culture deals with the shared assumptions (or deeper beliefs), values, and norms that lead to patterns of behavior within the organization. Persistent problems tend to be kept in place by covert assumptions, values, and norms that go unchallenged. Cultural norms, seen from a historical perspective, develop in order to solve problems. Later on, when conditions have changed, these norms become problems themselves.

> EXAMPLE: At UIA the mountains of paper constitute a symptom of deeper cultural issues. In UIA there has been a history of distrust between management, including supervisors, and workers. Paper has become a way of managing distrust. It enables people to avoid direct verbal contact with one another, to keep others off their backs, and to protect themselves (the CYA syndrome). Both leadership and the quality of lateral relationships need to be explored.

Like other companies, if UIA is to manage problems like this, it must explore and manage its culture.

ACTION IN STEP I-A:
DATA GATHERING AS INTERVENTION

The very identification of problems (together with their causes) and of opportunities can stimulate immediate action. Once problems and/or opportunities are identified, it is clear what needs to be done to manage the former and develop the latter. The very process of data gathering can stir people up and provide incentives for action.

> EXAMPLE: UIA hires a group of consultants to help them in their renewal efforts. In the interviews, people are asked what problems and opportunities they see and what they need in order to do their jobs better. At the end of the interviews, people are asked what they can do themselves *right away*, without asking permission from anyone, to manage the problems or develop the opportunities they have identified. This gets people thinking in action terms right from the start of the renewal project and produces an amazing number of system-enhancing actions. It seems as if people merely need to be given minimal encouragement to act.

Asking people what they can do immediately to make things better is not the same as forcing them into precipitous and ill-advised action. Most people have more power to act positively than they use. This reserve power is commonly used for self-protection. Moat-building behavior increases personal security at the cost of system efficiency and effectiveness. At any rate, it is important that system-enhancing action start immediately, even if some of the actions are merely symbolic of the will of the institution to better itself.

6

Shadow Side

Step I-B:
Challenging Blind Spots and Developing New Perspectives

If companies and institutions are to *do* things differently, they must often begin by *seeing* things differently. This means they must be open to be challenged by both people and events to develop new, more realistic, and more creative perspectives on business, organizational, managerial, and leadership realities.

The Names Given to the Process of Challenging. There are many names for the process of helping members of the organization develop the kinds of awareness and understanding that help them manage problems and develop opportunities: seeing things more clearly, getting the picture, getting insights, developing new perspectives, spelling out implications, perception transformation, developing new frames of reference, looking for meaning, perception shifting, seeing the bigger picture, frame breaking, developing different angles, seeing things in context, rethinking, getting a more objective view, interpreting, overcoming blind spots, analyzing, second-level learning, double-loop learning (Argyris, 1982), reframing, thinking creatively, reconceptualizing, discovery, having an "ah-hah" experience, developing a new outlook, getting rid of distortions, relabeling, making connections, paradigm shifts, and others. All of these imply some new kind of awareness that did not exist previously and which is needed or useful in order to engage in situation-improving action. But just as creativity is useful insofar as it leads to innovation, so new perspectives are useful insofar as they lead to changed patterns of behavior toward self, others, and the environment. Challenge is directed, not just to new forms of awareness, but to new forms of action.

"Shifting paradigms"

The Pervasiveness of Blind Spots. Organizations, like people, develop blind spots. While outside consultants can help organizations identify and deal with various forms of myopia, the best organizations, realizing that blind spots, like rust, accumulate in the natural course of events and impair the effectiveness of the system, build in self-monitoring systems. But even the best can be helped by objective outsiders from time to time to identify and challenge blind spots. Figure 6-1 indicates that dealing with a system's blind spots is a critical challenge in the management of change.

EXAMPLE: Whereas top managers in UIA saw the implementation of a performance planning and appraisal system (PPA) as an excellent vehicle not only for getting the best from the staff of the airline but also for improving morale, they tended to see PPA as a managerial tool involving communication that was principally top down. This was a blind spot for top managers because one of the major causes of dissatisfaction among middle managers and staff was the lack of bottom-up communication. Excellent ideas for improving both business performance and QWL went begging because of a managerial culture of arrogance and nonlistening.

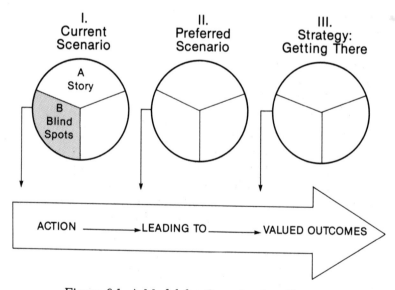

Figure 6-1. A Model for Organization Change

On the other hand, middle managers tended to see PPA as an added burden that offered them nothing. A consultant pointed out that one of the main reasons why PPA systems were successful was the kind of communication they fostered between different levels of the organization. Both senior and middle managers needed a completely different view of the function of communication in the organization. The new PPA system needed to be a change in the communication culture of UIA and not just an organizational change.

In this case top managers have their set of blind spots, while middle managers have theirs. The covert culture of an organization is often a hot bed of blind spots and therefore an ideal, if difficult, target for challenge.

Even a country's national culture, affecting as it does both business and organizational practices, may itself need challenging. Walden (1986) states:

> Britain could be a major force in the contemporary capitalist world. The reason that it is not has little to do with systems. It is a failure of individuals conditioned to lack ambition, taught to flinch from the struggle for excellence, and imprisoned by a false view of national history. Our culture is dominated by defeatists. . . . The lack of vision, undue caution, insufficient expertise, are not the sole preserve of industrial managers. They absorb these attitudes from the society around them. (p. 12)

Marketing is one of the commercial areas where Britain has fallen behind. In fact, as Marcom (1987) notes, "commercial" is almost a dirty word. He further states:

> Traditionally, the gentlemanly British executive hasn't paid much attention to marketing basics. That indifference didn't matter much when Britain was selling to a captive empire and held a technological lead. Today it is costly. (p. 1)

At least until recently, marketing and selling have not been well regarded in Britain. The university system channels their best graduates into the professions. A major polling firm in Britain says that the first career choice for university graduates is finance, followed by press and broadcasting. A business school has been established at Oxford only recently. Industry is still not respectable for the "best and brightest." Alcoholics Anonymous has long challenged the "stinkin' thinkin'" of those who would be defeated by alcohol. Corporations, institutions, agencies, and entire societies have their own brands of stinkin' thinkin'.

Developing New Perspectives. In a more positive vein, Step I-B deals with developing new, more creative perspectives to take the place of blind spots. The person in the company or institution capable of translating blind spots into new, more creative perspectives can be worth his or her weight in gold. Take the case of Corning Glass Works (see Trachtenberg, 1986a).

EXAMPLE: In 1982, after thirteen straight years of growth, the consumer products division of Corning Glass began to slip. A number of blind spots underlay the slide. First, lower-cost, high-quality, and more stylish imports began to flood in from Japan and Taiwan. Second, Corning managed to overlook one of the fastest growing product lines—microwave cookware. This market went from nothing to $500 million almost overnight. To make matters worse, Corning's products were suitable for use in microwaves, but they did not mount a campaign to let consumers know that until early in 1985. Corning did not get around to introducing a specific microwave product line until 1985. Until 1984 Corning rarely did a market study and rarely sampled consumer preferences. As Trachtenberg (1986a, p. 173) notes, Corning "turned its back on its consumers and on product trends transforming the industry. Complacency breeds hard lessons, the clearest of which is, it is far easier to lose market share than to regain it."

What we see here is the opposite of a culture of vigilance and its cost.

Companies lose their creative edge when they allow life to become too cozy, the world to become too narrow, their organizations to become more important than their businesses, their stakeholders to be overlooked or undercontrolled, and themselves to become mired down in blind spots. In religion the adage *Ecclesia semper reformanda* (the church is *always* in need of reformation) expresses a truth that should not be lost on the corporate world, education, government, and human-service institutions. A culture of self-challenge together with a culture of vigilance characterizes the best systems. Most change projects move forward because agents of change

parallel to adaptive vs. nonadaptive cultures in Kotter + Heskett engage in a judicious combination of support and challenge. Support without challenge becomes effete; challenge without support leads to adversarial relationships.

Since blind spots are, by definition, outside awareness, both individuals and organizations can from time to time benefit from the views of outsiders. Outsiders can have the kind of objectivity needed to cut through nonsense. One way of doing this is to visit or at least review the experience of the *exemplars* in any given field—the organizations or institutions that are the most creative and successful.

EXAMPLE: In an unparalleled move, the boards of trustees of a number of different international development institutes got together to compare notes and to discover ways of being more helpful to the institutions they governed. During the course of their discussions, a number of blind spots common to such institutions surfaced. For instance, they tended to see themselves as unique. Doing so had meant not just ignoring, but even discounting "best practice" in the business world.

The result? They were less effectively managed than they might have been. The new perspective? The best companies may well have a great deal to teach us. Some of these institutes adopted up-to-date management-development programs and benefitted from "best practice" in the business world without losing their special character.

Narrowness on the part of any enterprise—whether profit or not-for-profit—can be deadly. On the other hand, developing new perspectives is not the same as pursuing business, organizational, or managerial fads.

Blind spots are often difficult to challenge precisely because they are cultural in nature, rooted in covert assumptions, values, and norms that are both organizational and personal (Egan, 1985, 1986, 1988). The mere existence of blind spots does not imply ill will. However, those individuals and organizations that admit the universality of self-deception (see Goleman, 1985) as self-protection against painful truths are more likely to engage in self-monitoring and even welcome painful, but useful truths, whatever their source. Change and problem solving at their best are imaginative processes. Challenging blind spots at the service of new, more creative perspectives is an essential part of that process.

AREAS CALLING FOR CHALLENGE

Model A offers a check list for areas within a company or institution that need challenging. That is, for a company or institution to manage its problems or develop its opportunities, its members may have to challenge its conceptions of its markets, the way it understands and manages its environment, its mission, its business philosophy, its human resource policies and practices, the current mix of major categories of products and services, the value and quality of its products or services, the quality of its customer service, its work programs, the management of its finances and other material resources; its structure, the raison d'etre for each of it units, the mix of jobs and responsibilities, the effectiveness of each of its units, the competence and compatibility of its workers, the quality of teamwork among units and individuals, the quality of its communication processes, its management, the quality of its leadership, and its effectiveness in managing its culture and other forms of system arationality.

Processes and procedures that often call for challenging in the change process itself include the following:

Surrender vs. Control

Blind Spots and Restatement of Problems and Opportunities

underpinning

There are two broad categories of problem solvers: adapters and innovators. Adapters overcome or adapt to (that is, cope with) the problem. Innovators, on the other hand, engage in problem finding, question the very definition of the problem, and try to reformulate problems in terms of opportunities. It is often useful to restate problems and opportunities from different perspectives.

For instance, one of the brightest members of the finance department in United International Airways, in discussing the flotation of UIA stock, says, "The issue is not how to float a new UIA stock offering; that is a strategy, a means to an end. The real issue is how to keep the airline financially flexible and robust. There are a whole range of strategies we have not considered."

One of the reasons that problems are not managed well is that change agents have blind spots that prevent them from seeing problems and opportunities creatively. Here are some challenging questions to help in identifying problems and searching for opportunities (the work of step I-A):

- What are we overlooking in the definition of this problem of stating this opportunity? *leaving*
- In what ways can we challenge the assumptions underlying the problem or opportunity as currently stated?
- How many different ways can we define the problem or frame the opportunity?
- What biases or vested interests do we have that keep us from seeing this problem or opportunity objectively?
- In what ways is the past keeping us from a different view of the problem or leading us astray in our search for opportunities? *UNDISCUSSABLES*
- What unpleasant realities are we trying to avoid in the current definition of the problem or the framing of the opportunity?
- How can the problem or opportunity be restated at a more abstract or comprehensive level?
- In what ways might it be useful to divide the problem or opportunity into different parts?

Old frames need to be broken so that the problem or opportunity and therefore the preferred scenario can be reframed. Blind spots must be challenged so that new, more objective, more creative, and more useful perspectives can be developed.

Challenging the Ownership of Problems and Opportunities

Ultimately, problems and opportunities must be defined in terms of the outcomes and behaviors that are in the control of the change agents. If the people in UIA cabin crew services persist in saying, "Our problem is that the people in catering are not doing things right," then the problem is not stated in solvable terms. On the other hand, if they say: "Our problem is that we have not been working collaboratively with catering, telling them about the problems that arise, giving them helpful feedback on their services, and offering suggestions based on passenger comments," then something can be done about it. Both individuals and organizational units tend to protect themselves by stating problems in terms of what *others* are or are not doing. They need to be challenged to translate problems and opportunities into their own behavior.

Challenging the Tendency to Blame the Environment and Circumstances

Blaming outside forces is one common form of resistance to problem management, innovation, and opportunity development. Outside forces may well interfere seriously with efforts to change and set limits on the degree of change, but the tendency to blame such forces needs to be challenged.

> EXAMPLE: When asked why its efforts kept falling short, the marketing department of UIA had traditionally said things like this:
>
> - "The surge in oil prices that led to the fuel surcharge has hurt us."
> - "Lingering fear about terrorism keeps the market depressed."
> - "Delta has upgraded its fleet, and people like flying on new planes."
> - "Consumer tastes are changing more rapidly than ever before, and it is practically impossible to hit a moving target."
> - "Government deregulation has made markets too jittery. The usual approaches to marketing are now only partially successful."

In a word, what should have been seen as challenges were being offered as excuses. No wonder top management at UIA came to the conclusion that it was time for a change in the marketing department. This kind of excuse making is common in many different kinds of companies and institutions. After American Telephone & Telegraph had divested itself of the Bell Companies, people in both organizations—when asked why things were taking so long or why mistakes were being made—routinely mumbled something about "divestiture." The best systems strive to cope with and overcome environmental obstacles rather than use them as excuses. In 1986 the per-capita income in Korea exceeded that of Argentina. The latter is rich in natural resources, whereas South Korea—like Japan—is poor in oil, coal, and agricultural lands (see Forbes, 1986).

The blaming process goes on all the time in companies and institutions, standing in the way of immediate problem-managing action.

> EXAMPLE: After the jet engine fire that led to the death of thirty-four passengers, the relatives of those who had died and the survivors blamed UIA. A number of UIA people started to look for parties to blame. The maintenance people pointed fingers at the manufacturers and to pilots who had failed to report engine anomalies. Some executives blamed the FAA for not dealing with the engine problem effectively. However, UIA's CEO, convinced that an organization in which individuals and units spend time looking for culprits is an organization in trouble, called a halt to this and established task forces to examine procedures in the maintenance department, to work with the manufacturer, and to deal with the FAA on larger issues of engine safety. He challenged the defensiveness of the airline and instead urged key players to *action.*

Energy needs to be poured, not into blaming others, circumstances, environmental factors, and whatever else can be added to the list, but into finding creative ways of *managing* these factors. In step I-B basically three things are challenged: forms of thinking that are self-defeating (prejudices, biases, ignorance, second guessing, and the like), acting in self-defeating ways (such as blaming others), and failures to act (indecision, procrastination, and the like).

CHALLENGE AT EVERY STAGE
AND STEP OF THE CHANGE MODEL

Organizations have blind spots with respect to the way they go about managing problems and developing opportunities and these, too, need to be challenged. For instance, some people underuse parts of the model that call for vision, insight, and imagination, while others underuse systematic data gathering. Some overuse the problem identification phases of the model, while others leap into imprudent action. The model should be used situationally. That is, given the problem or opportunity, the change agent can ask, "Which steps of the change process will be most useful here? What steps have the greatest potential leverage? How effectively are people using the steps of the change process?" Key players may have to be challenged to:

- Consider what actions might be taken right from the beginning of the change process (Action Bias).
- Reconceptualize problems and opportunities in terms of fact rather than opinion and hearsay (I-A).
- Move beyond mere self-interest in identifying high-impact problems and opportunities (I-C).
- Put aside preconceptions and biases in brainstorming preferred scenario possibilities (II-A).
- Avoid vague and unrealistic goals, objectives, and agendas (II-B).
- Search for the incentives that can command commitment to new agendas (II-C).
- Use their imagination to find creative strategies for accomplishing goals (III-A).
- Become realistic about the resources to manage problems and develop opportunities (III-B).
- Develop the discipline called for by action plans (III-C).
- Move beyond both inertia and entropy to the kind of sustained action that leads to the accomplishment of system-enhancing goals (Action Bias).

A culture of challenging is completely different from whining and carping. It is part of the culture of vigilance discussed in step I-A.

7

Step I-C:
Leverage—the Search for High-Impact Problems and Opportunities

The full organizational story may reveal a whole range of organizational problems, deficits, and unused opportunities. Or the problems and opportunities may be few but complex and far-reaching. Since everything cannot be done at once, it is essential that high-priority problems or opportunities be chosen for attention. Companies and institutions, once they have reviewed their stories and studied the vigilance grid, must ask themselves, "What problems and/or opportunities, if addressed, will give us the greatest return on our investment of time, personnel, and money?" This step deals with sorting problems and opportunities, finding points of leverage, and gathering data at the service of action-oriented clarity and specificity.

THE GOALS OF STEP I-C

The following three goals, although they can be distinguished conceptually, overlap in practice, just as step I-C can overlap with steps I-A and I-B. The nonlinear use of Model A must always be kept in mind.

1. **Initial Screening.** A judgment needs to be made whether the problems or opportunities revealed in step I-A merit serious consideration. Some problems solve themselves with the passage of time; some

opportunities develop naturally over time. For instance, the quality of food in the cafeteria at corporate headquarters of UIA could probably be improved, but at the moment it does not merit serious consideration.

2. The Search for Leverage. Since not all concerns in a complex problem/opportunity situation can be dealt with at once, a second goal is to decide which problems or opportunities should be addressed first. The issue is *leverage*, return on investment of time and other resources, cost versus benefit. For instance, investing in commuter airlines and turning them into United International Airways Express networks is a business opportunity not to be missed. It needs immediate attention.

3. Clarification. Once a problem or opportunity is chosen for attention, it needs to be explored and clarified. The third goal of this step is to understand the problem or opportunity with the kind of specificity that allows both system-enhancing outcomes and outcome-producing action strategies to be identified. However, no matter how well we scrutinize them, some problems and opportunities do not reveal themselves all at once. They need to be worked with and are clearly understood through a combination of analysis and action. Consider the fire in one of the engines of a UIA jet on takeoff that led to the death of thirty-four passengers. Since other airlines have experienced problems with the same engine model and since UIA's fleet has many of them, UIA needs to work closely with the manufacturer and with its own maintenance department to discover the precise causes of the malfunction. Figure 7-1 adds the final step to Stage I.

INITIAL SCREENING

What happens when there is a lack of a culture of vigilance and when indecision keeps a corporation from choosing high-leverage problems to manage and opportunities to pursue?

EXAMPLE: One of UIA's largest competitors was facing a beleaguering number of problems. Deregulation produced a bevy of smaller

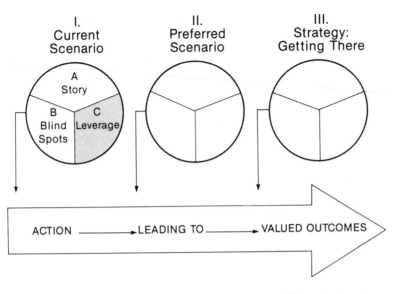

Figure 7-1. A Model for Organization Change

nonunion airlines with much lower costs. These competitors were taking business away by offering lower fares. Unions were balking against further givebacks. Both pilots and flight attendants were threatening to strike. A number of refinancing programs had taken place, but now creditors were pushing for more drastic austerity measures. There were serious internal disagreements. Some thought that the CEO should step down. A sense of crisis prevailed in which trust had all but disappeared. Predators were circling, assessing takeover possibilities.

The problems here were so overwhelming that bankruptcy and reorganization or a takeover might have seemed to be the only way out. Indecision prevailed and things were allowed to get out of hand. Had some of these critical issues been addressed with greater imagination earlier, this mess might have been avoided. How did it all end? A hostile takeover that satisfied no one took place.

No-Go Decisions. Organizational problem solving and change are expensive in terms of both financial and human costs. They should not be undertaken lightly. Although relatively little is said in the literature about screening, that is, making a decision as to whether any given problem situation or opportunity deserves attention, in practice the best organizations let many insignificant problems and unpromising opportunities fall by the wayside. That is, a no-go decision is seen as the best option. On the other hand, some organizations waste time on inconsequential problems and opportunities. The decision not to deal with a low-leverage problem or opportunity can:

- Keep the members of the organization from wasting time, effort, and money.
- Delay attention until a more suitable time.
- Provide the time needed to protect and consolidate gains from current or previous change efforts.
- Provide the organization with an opportunity to discover that some problems can take care of themselves.
- Prevent members of the organization from pretending to deal with a problem or opportunity when no effective way of doing so currently exists.

Of course, poorly executed screening can lead to premature judgments about the seriousness of problems and the potential of opportunities.

Readiness for Change. A second screening issue relates to the *commitment* of the organization to do something about its problems and opportunities and its *ability* to do so. This means that there must be some reasonable hope that key members of the organization are willing to do more than merely talk about their concerns. Or it means that there is some reasonable hope that a key member will become productively involved in the change effort. At one end of the continuum is a willingness on the part of change agents, whether managers or consultants, to work with clients who give little or no evidence of a commitment to working for change. At the other end of the continuum is a tendency to ignore the understandable hesitancies of clients to commit themselves to change and to throw down the gauntlet: "Come back when you want to do something about it." Experienced change agents do not opt for either end point of this continuum. Appendix B presents a check list, developed by Pfeiffer and Jones (1978), that can be used by change agents to assess a system's readiness for change.

CRITERIA FOR CHOOSING HIGH-LEVERAGE PROBLEMS OR OPPORTUNITIES

When it comes to change, sometimes corporations and institutions merely need to do something, anything. More often they need to do the right thing. This means choosing high-priority problems or opportunities for attention. This is especially true if a problem situation or opportunity is complex. The Pareto Principle, applied to managing, suggests that managers get about 80 percent of their results from about 20 percent of their activities. The issue is leverage. The same principle can also be applied to organizational problem solving and opportunity development. Which problems, which opportunities, if attended to, will move us most quickly and substantively away from deficit, disaster, or defeat and toward excellence?

The following principles of leverage can be used by change agents to guide the company or institution in question in its choice of concerns or opportunities for immediate attention. These principles are interrelated so that more than one might apply at the same time.

• **Business Versus Organization.** Other things being equal, choose a business—rather than an organizational—problem or opportunity (for reasons outlined in Egan, 1988).

EXAMPLE: Since load factor is critical to UIA's profitability, two of its immediate business concerns are establishing two more hubs, one in the Southeast and one in the West, and getting commuter airlines to feed these hubs. These opportunities need immediate attention.

This does not mean that there are no critical organizational concerns or opportunities that might need immediate attention. However, in choosing organizational problems, make sure that they are linked to substantive business concerns.

• **Ownership and Control.** Determine whether or not the problem or opportunity belongs to you or to your unit. If not, refer it to those who need to take ownership of it. *Start* with a problem or opportunity that is under your control, not one that demands intensive interaction with other units (unless the interunit problem constitutes a crisis).

- **Crises.** If the problem is urgent or constitutes a crisis for the organization, attend to it immediately. At least do whatever is necessary to defuse the crisis. Once the crisis is defused, use the following as criteria to establish priorities.

- **Problems/Opportunities with Substance.** Choose problems rather than symptoms, real opportunities rather than flash-in-the-pan ideas. On the other hand, do not overlook small problems that can easily grow into large ones or small possibilities that can be turned into substantive opportunities.

- **Stress.** Give priority to problems or undeveloped opportunities that are causing you, your customers, and/or the members of the organization pain or discomfort. If people are hurting, they are motivated to use their resources to grapple with the problem.

- **Enthusiasm.** Begin with a problem or opportunity (or some part of either) that you and the members of the organization are enthusiastic about or at least are willing to work on. This means reviewing your own incentives and theirs for addressing these issues. Incentives can include problem/opportunity clarity, agreement on the definition of the problem or the formulation of an opportunity, and agreement about the need for action.

- **Spread Effect.** Begin with a problem or opportunity which, if managed or developed, will take care of other problems or lead to overall improvement in the work unit. This is known as the *spread effect.* Review the problems or opportunities you face and see if there are certain themes that run through them. Then tackle the thematic elements that have the most utility.

- **Ease.** Begin with an easy problem, one that can be handled quickly and with a minimum expenditure of resources. Or begin with a simpler part of a complex problem. This helps create a problem-solving and innovation-developing mood in the organization. Success acts as an incentive for addressing more difficult problems and opportunities.

• **Visibility.** If the problem or opportunity is visible to the members of your unit, its very visibility may act as an incentive for solving it or developing it. If it is visible to other units in the organization, political considerations may suggest your addressing it quickly.

• **Comprehensiveness.** Other things being equal, the more people affected, the greater the urgency to address the problem. If both customers and members of the organization are affected, the problem or opportunity takes on a greater urgency.

• **Chronicity.** Recurring problems may need immediate attention because they drain the unit's resources. The trouble with chronic problems is that they are so familiar that the ways in which they drain resources go unnoticed. Recall UIA's culture-related "mountains of paper" problem discussed earlier.

• **Cost/Benefit Ratio.** Focus on a problem or opportunity for which the benefits will outweigh the costs. Include both financial and psychological costs.

This list is not exhaustive. Other equally relevant criteria could be added. The point is that some system is needed to sort out problems and opportunities.

Ordinarily, problems and opportunities chosen for attention will conform to a number of the above criteria. This is the case with UIA's choice of an organizational issue for immediate attention.

EXAMPLE: Since UIA has just developed and announced a new mission statement and since, unlike many organizations, efforts are being made to communicate the mission to everyone in every unit of the airline, it is seen as a golden opportunity for doing something about the performance-appraisal system. One of the reasons the company has been adrift has been its reliance on controls imposed by managers rather than controls embedded in the workers themselves. The appraisal system has been a joke because it has not been tied to effective performance planning and feedback. A total performance planning-feedback-appraisal system is needed. UIA knows that a great deal of quality of work life has to be rooted in pride of performance. Since many people have had vague work objectives, have received no feedback, and have seen appraisal as a waste of time, pride in performance has been, at best, a hit-and-miss affair. However, since an effectively operating performance planning and appraisal system seems to address so many problems and to lead to the development of so many opportunities, it is given high priority.

The performance planning and appraisal system (PPA) is chosen because it is seen as an opportunity of substance, it is highly visible, it can be used to manage a wide range of problems and develop a wide range of opportunities, and—if done well—its costs outweigh its benefits. PPA has three "moments":

1. Collaborative planning and objective setting between manager or supervisor and worker.

2. Ongoing confirmatory and corrective feedback.

3. The semiannual or annual appraisal of performance against objectives.

All of these involve the kind of face-to-face communication that most managers and supervisors at UIA find difficult. Therefore, if a new PPA system is going to work, the underlying organizational-culture problems discussed in Step I-A will have to be addressed at the same time.

EXPLORATION AND CLARIFICATION: MAKING PROBLEMS AND OPPORTUNITIES CRISP

Once clients decide to what they would like to give their attention, the next goal is exploration and clarification of problems and opportunities. Problems and opportunities that are clearly formulated and defined are easier to manage. The search for clarity and definition should, however, be focused: it is not a question of gathering facts for the sake of facts.

Outcome-Related Data

The organization does not need data or facts that are dreary, facts that beget more facts, facts that are never ending, facts that go nowhere, much less facts that befuddle, facts that mislead. Rather it needs facts with an edge, facts that will get the enterprise somewhere, facts that have the seeds of new scenarios and action strategies in them, information that is outcome related. Geneen (Geneen & Moscow, 1984) insisted on "unshakable" facts. For Geneen unshakable facts were not "apparent facts," "assumed facts," "reported facts," "hoped-for facts," or "accepted facts," (p. 97) and he felt that serious decisions could not be based on them:[1]

> Whole trains of events and decisions for an entire management can be put in motion in the wrong direction—with inevitable loss of money, time, and morale—by one "unfactual fact," accepted by or submitted by YOU—however unintentional. The highest art of professional management requires the literal ability to "small" a "real fact" from all others—and moreover to have the temerity, intellectual curiosity, guts and/or plain impoliteness, if necessary, to be sure that what you do have is indeed what we will call an "unshakable fact." (p. 97)

Amassing facts is exploration. It is often necessary. But sifting out "Geneen-type" facts is an exercise in problem or opportunity *clarification*. Part of the clarification process is separating biased facts from objective facts:[2]

> The truth is that the so-called "facts" are almost always colored by the bias of the man presenting them. . . . Salesmen will always reflect what their customers are telling them, and they tend to exaggerate the parameters either on the up or on the down side; marketing men put their faith in statistical analyses of what the market should be for your products, with little regard for what your customers are saying; engineers usually have an idea for a new product (which may or may not be what the market or the customers want at that time); someone else will have a dream of what could happen if only. . .and someone else will have a nightmare about all the things that could go wrong. The manager in charge must take the "facts" presented by each of them, strip away the biases, including his own, and try to get a true

---

[1]Excerpt from *Managing* by Harold S. Geneen and Alvin Moscow. Copyright © 1984 by Harold S. Geneen and Alvin Moscow, Inc. Reprinted by permission of Doubleday, a division of Bantam, Doubleday, Dell Publishing Group, Inc.

[2]Ibid.

picture of what is involved. . . . As more and more different sources report the "facts" to you, the reality of the situation (or as close to it as you can come) will emerge. (pp. 116-117)

For Geneen, seeing the situation (the problem, the opportunity) clearly made the decision clear and easy. However, even he admits that not all situations can be spelled out in terms of unshakable facts, but decision makers should know precisely what is clear and what is vague and proceed accordingly.

Creativity in Seeking Causes

Once certain problems are identified, the solutions are quite clear. In other cases, solutions are developed only after the causes of the problem are identified. Finding possible causes is exploration; finding actual causes is clarification. This requires "thinking backward," which, at its best is a creative process; it is not just a question of digging up the right data. Einhorn and Hogarth (1987) put it this way:

> Thinking backward is largely intuitive and suggestive; it tends to be diagnostic and requires judgment. It involves looking for patterns, making links between seemingly unconnected events, testing possible chains of causation to explain an event, and finding a metaphor or a theory to help in looking forward. (p. 66)

As we have seen, UIA comes to realize that a number of its most persistent problems are rooted in the past that is still present, that is, its organizational culture.

In summary, the search for data and data analysis should serve rather than drive the problem-management and opportunity-development processes. Both accuracy and imagination are called for.

SEARCHING FOR LEVERAGE
THROUGHOUT THE CHANGE PROCESS

The search for leverage is not restricted to Step I-C. First, the larger question is: Given the entire change model, what parts of it will provide the most leverage in helping the organization manage some problem situation or develop some opportunity more effectively? Second, Steps II-B and III-B are decision-making steps:

- II-B: Which elements of a preferred scenario should be included?
- III-B: Which strategies should be chosen to implement the vision?

Decision making has four components:

1. **Alternatives.** Decision makers have a set of alternatives for action. The more clearly these are known the better. UIA says, "This is the era of givebacks so we can 'tough it out' with the unions, or we can use this as an opportunity to establish a collaborative style with them."

2. **Consequences.** Ideally, decision makers know the consequences of the alternatives identified. UIA explores the pluses and minuses of each of these approaches to its unions.

3. **Values.** Decision makers compare alternative consequences of action in terms of their value. UIA explores the consequences of these two different approaches to its unions in terms, let us say, of the new "people" values it wants to promote.

4. **Criteria.** Decision makers have criteria or rules by which to select a single alternative or a set of alternatives on the basis of their preferred consequences. UIA uses business and organizational criteria (business goals, finances, the negative consequences of strikes, and so forth), permeated by its business and other values, to choose its approach to the unions.

The decision-making process suffers to the degree that any one of these elements is defective. For instance, the search for alternatives might be incomplete, serious consequences may be overlooked, alternatives might be inadequately compared in terms of their consequences, espoused values may be put aside, and the criteria chosen may be superficial. Decision making is riddled with arationality. For instance, far too many decisions are based on taste rather than data. Biases, interdepartmental rivalries, powerful personalities, traditions that have outlived their usefulness, the covert culture, panic, and a host of other "shadow-side" factors skew the process. Accepting the fact that decision making is an uphill battle is a giant step toward making sure that decisions serve the common good.

STAGE II

THE PREFERRED SCENARIO

Overview

Developing a Range of Possible Futures

Turning a Scenario into a Viable Agenda

Commitment—Linking the Agenda to Action

Quand le rêve est devenue realité,
il faut changer de rêve.

G. Moréas, *Un flic de l'interieur.*

When a dream becomes reality,
it's time to change the dream.

8

An Overview of Stage II: The Preferred Scenario

Stage II is, in many ways, the heart of the change process. It is the point at which imagination is most critical. Once the organization sees the deficit or the unused opportunity, the next step is not to look for ways of managing the problem or exploiting the opportunity. The questions to be asked are, "What would the problem look like, if solved? What would the opportunity look like, if developed? No matter what the organization, the organizational unit, the project, or the program looks like now, what do we want it to look like?" Stage II does not deal with strategies or means; it deals rather with accomplishments, achievements, outcomes. The ability of an organization to picture what it needs and wants is priceless. Stage II has three distinct steps:

A. Developing a range of preferred scenarios or preferred possibilities that can be "packaged" in a variety of ways so as to constitute a preferred scenario.

B. Establishing criteria for evaluating and choosing alternative possibilities in order to establish a viable agenda.

C. Getting the commitment of the organization to the new scenario.

A. Develop a range of preferred possibilities or scenarios. Against the background of the assessment done in Stage I, the following questions are asked: "What would this problem look like if it were being managed effectively? What would this key opportunity look like were it fully developed? What would our company or institution look like if it were an exemplar in the field? What would our organization look like if it were really serving the business needs of our enterprise?"

EXAMPLE: The energy department of an investment bank was demoralized because of the catastrophic changes caused by the collapse of the oil market. Instead of being the darlings of the bank as they were before the oil crisis, they now felt like second-class citizens. Cutting back was the order of the day. A couple of the best people had left. The manager of the department volunteered his department as a case during a management-development program on change.

He was asked to picture his department the way he would like to see it. He said that it would have a new mission, one still related to energy but also to the current realities of the energy industry. His staff would be out looking for new markets and helping clients come up with creative energy projects, seeking customers out instead of waiting for customers to contact them. They would be entrepreneurial within the limits set for them by upper management, looking for energy possibilities in other loan projects. This would mean that his staff would be interacting much more with other departments of the bank. They would be working to improve the image of the energy department within the bank. All of this would lead to renewed enthusiasm and an improved quality of work life for him and his staff.

The manager in this example went on to spell out a preferred future in much greater detail. He left the seminar with every intention of repeating the process with his staff.

B. Choose the best possibilities and develop criteria to package them in a realistic preferred scenario or agenda. In this step creativity is turned into innovation. Criteria for a viable agenda such as clarity and specificity are applied. The following example is based on an article in *Administrative Management* (Los Angeles County Public Administrator, 1986):

EXAMPLE: Workers in the city of Glendale, Arizona, saddled with an aging computer used only for accounting, clamored for office-automation equipment. They had a vision of equipment that could handle word processing, administrative management, spreadsheets, and project management, as well as data process applications that would service finance and budget, payroll, personnel, police investigations, and similar needs. A feasibility study helped the information systems department turn a vision into a realistic agenda.

The department proposed a DATA General MV/8000 and two MN/4000 minicomputers together with a digital PBX phone system. The integrated computer system would provide processing capability for 150 users in the city's various departments. There would be standard software packages for data and word processing, but these would be complemented by in-house software programs tailored to meet the needs of specific departments (for instance, police investigations). The computer hardware and software would cost $700,000 and the PBX system would cost $315,000—well within the city's budget, considering the savings that would be generated. A timetable was established to phase in the terminals. The number of terminals would grow from nine to 150 over eighteen months.

Visions, however, are not enough. After brainstorming possibilities, a realistic preferred scenario or agenda needs to be established. In the above case, specificity and realism of the information systems department proved to be a driving force. The proposal was adopted and completed within the scheduled time frame.

C. Present the agenda and get commitment to it from key stakeholders. Make sure that key players are buying into the preferred scenario. This work can start early by making sure that key players are involved in the identification of both problems and opportunities and the development of a range of new-scenario possibilities.

EXAMPLE: A small computer company was in danger of going under because of the sustained downturn in the computer industry. The president, after interviewing formally and informally a large number of employees, worked out with some of his key managers a preferred scenario built around survival. The survival scenario, of course, had some grim parts. Costs needed to be cut severely, inventories had to be lowered, the work force needed to be trimmed, salaries had to be reduced by about 10 percent, and people had to be reassigned to marketing and sales from other departments. The preferred scenario also called for moving into the software business through the sale of software products already developed for in-house use and an option to receive partial salary payment through stock in the company.

His presentation of the new scenario was well received because employees understood that they were facing a crisis not entirely of their own making; they felt that his proposals were eminently practical and fair; they appreciated being consulted; and they were given some hope in terms of surviving the downturn, becoming financial stakeholders through the stock-option plan, and moving into a new business (software). There was a sense that everyone was going to pitch in to reach the goals outlined in the survival scenario.

It is necessary to present a preferred scenario that is clear, detailed, and appealing. Even the grim scenario outlined above was appealing because it was based on consultation, it was fair, and it offered hope. However, once that is done, *it is also essential to create a climate of learning and problem solving around the agenda.* This, as seen in Model A, is a primary leadership function.

THE USE OF MODEL A
IN STAGE II

Just as Model A can serve as a template for organizational assessment, so can it be used to stimulate thinking about a better business and organizational future. Model A deals with the pragmatics of excellence, that is, the process of designing effectiveness into the system. Change projects are, from one point of view, exercises in system redesign. The questions in Appendix A, taken from Model A (Egan, 1988), can serve as stimuli for thinking more creatively about the company or institution's business, organization, management, and leadership.

9

Step II-A: Developing a Range of Possible Futures

This step—as important as it is—was until recently found in relatively few problem-solving and organization-change models. Most leap from the clarification of the problem to what are called *solutions*. The term "solution" is ambiguous. In many problem-solving models it refers to the actions that need to be taken to manage the problem or develop the opportunity. However, solution can also mean what will be *in place* once these strategies are implemented. That is, the term *solution*, in its deepest meaning refers to the preferred scenario, to outcomes, to accomplishments. The distinction is important. Cohen, March, and Olsen (1972), in a classic article, note that in premature problem solving and change, people with "solutions" in terms of pet ideas, projects, or whatever go out looking for places to use them, disregarding whether or not they fit the mission or preferred change scenario of the enterprise.

Step II-A, as noted in Figure 9-1, involves brainstorming possibilities related to a better future for the company or institution, a future in which the organization is renewed, the problem is solved, the opportunity is developed, the challenge is met. "What would this organization look like if it looked better?" is a powerful question because it helps organizations look beyond present difficulties and limitations and because it focuses on outcomes and accomplishments rather than strategies.

The following homey example makes it clear that specifying a preferred scenario is an activity that relates, not just to major change projects, but to all projects.

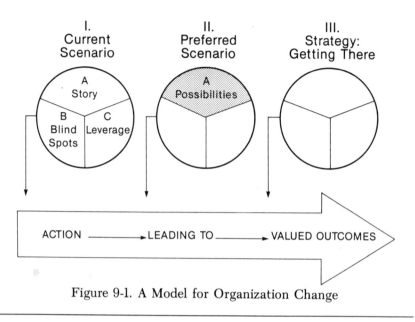

Figure 9-1. A Model for Organization Change

EXAMPLE: A newly created vice president of marketing of one of the Bell companies called and said he had picked his team and they were going to meet for the first time in about a month. He asked if I would come and facilitate the meeting. I responded, "First of all, I assume that it is your meeting and that I will be helping you facilitate it." "Well. . .yes, of course," was the reply. "Second," I said, "what would you like to see exist at the end of the meeting that will not exist at the beginning?" Silence. I waited. "That's a good question," he said. "That's an excellent question," said I, "one that needs to be answered to our mutual satisfaction if we are to strike a contract." The ensuing dialog led to the identification of several critical outcomes.

RENEWED INTEREST IN CREATIVITY

Current management and organization-effectiveness literature reflects a renewed interest in topics such as creativity, vision, intuition, imagination, and right-brain versus left-brain activity. Perhaps the "rational" manager is best fitted for steady-state companies or institutions in a steady-state environment. But companies and institutions battling turbulent environments need what Rowan (1986) calls "intuitive" managers. He interviewed dozens of CEOs in his research on the function of intuition in managerial decision making. He discovered that intuition is currently flourishing at the top of some very successful organizations and is coupled with fostering creativity in the organization:

> It takes a perceptive CEO, oftentimes one who remembers how freewheeling and exciting things were during his company's start-up days, to initiate remedial action [with a creative flair]. Nevertheless, any intuitive CEO can implement certain changes to help make the biggest corporation more sensitive to its creative people. Establishing autonomous subunits with their own budgets and profit centers encourages inventive, entrepreneurial spirit to bubble up from the bottom, and may even spark an occasional Eureka. The term "intrapreneurship," now in vogue, describes the setting up of small separate businesses within such behemoths as GM or IBM so talented employees can chance their dreams and possibly strike it rich without quitting. (p. 22)

When Norman Brown became CEO of Foote, Cone, and Belding (an advertising agency) in 1982, he set out to produce more innovative advertising. He used his own version of the "whole brain" theory as a kind of metaphor to get account executives ("left brains") and the creative people ("right brains") to engage in more effective teamwork at the service of innovation. In his view, too many great ideas were being wasted. The whole-brain theory seemed to act as a symbol and catalyst. In Spragins' (1986) words:

> The account team was tempted to make a commercial listing the fine ingredients in Sara Lee's bagels—a "low-involvement/rational" pitch, in whole-brain lingo. A little right-brain thinking, however, and they developed a more emotional pitch based on the fact that consumers said they eat Sara Lee products to indulge themselves. So Foote made a sensual ad that shows a woman savoring a bagel to the accompaniment of bump-and-grind music.

Sara Lee liked the ad, seeing it as getting at the "peculiar mystique" of the bagel eater. Change, problem solving, innovation, and opportunity development cry out for imagination, and yet the research shows that most of us use only a fraction of our imaginal resources. It is as if people needed permission to unfetter their imaginations.

SCENARIO BUILDING

[handwritten: managing for the future — being now what you will be]

Problems and unused opportunities can make members of organizations feel hemmed in and closed off. The goal of this step is to develop a range of new scenarios or a range of new-scenario possibilities. A scenario, as used here, is a picture or image of what the problem situation would look like if it were being managed more effectively or what an opportunity would look if it were developed. A scenario possibility is one part of the picture. Key members of the organization are helped to picture themselves in the future, managing a problem situation or some part of it, developing some opportunity, or putting some innovation in place. They are helped to see themselves engaging in patterns of behavior with outcomes that are more constructive than the outcomes of the patterns of behavior currently in place. Current leadership models emphasize the leader's ability to develop a vision. Bennis and Nanus (1985) state:

> To choose a direction, a leader must first have developed a mental image of a possible and desirable future state of the organization. This image, which we call *vision*, may be as vague as a dream or as precise as a goal or mission statement. The critical point is that a vision articulates a view of a realistic, credible, attractive future for the organization, a condition that is better in some important ways than what now exists. (p. 89)

Good managers "know the numbers," but leaders know that the whole truth is not found in the numbers. They know that a great deal of truth is found in pictures, in images of a better future. According to Naisbitt and Aburdene (1985):

> The first ingredient in re-inventing the corporation is a powerful vision—a whole new sense of where a company is going and how to get there. It is important to understand trends. . . but it is not enough. You must also discover the specific way that your company fits into the business environment. The company's vision becomes a catalytic force, an organizing principle for everything that the people in the corporation do. (p. 20)

This can be said of small companies and institutions as well as large; it can be said of units within the company or institution; it can be said of projects and programs within the units.

There are a number of questions that tend to stimulate the ability of the members of an organization to create new scenarios. Using questions like these to brainstorm should produce a list of preferred-scenario possibilities. Here are some questions together with the beginnings of answers:

- What would this company look like if it were functioning better?

  A company manufacturing specialty steel products: "It would have better overseas markets for the fine products it produces, especially in countries where the dollar has fallen sharply over the last year. We would be out there creating our markets instead of waiting for people to discover us."

- What patterns of behavior would disappear and what patterns would take their place?

  A computer company: "We would see the other units that we interact with in the organization as suppliers and customers and not as adversaries. Blaming behavior would be cut drastically. We would pursue internal customer relations as vigorously as we develop external customer relations. This would make us more efficient, contribute to the bottom line, and improve quality of work life."

- If this institution were a leader in its field, what would it look like?

  A university psychology department: "We would not have a clinical psychology program that is a carbon copy of all the others. We would be specializing in applied research. We would be challenging the taboos of our profession. Our graduates would be 'translators,' that is, professionals who do not necessarily do research but who stay in touch with basic research and who specialize in 'translating' this research into models, methods, and skills for practitioners. We would be turning out professionals more committed to serving the community than nurturing their profession."

- What accomplishments would be in place that are not in place now?

An airline: "We would have a comprehensive employee-assistance program in place. Cabin crew, because of its special needs would have a self-help program, which would include a 24-hour hotline and a walk-in center located at our major hub. Volunteers staffing the self-help program would be trained in basic counseling skills."

- What would this problem look like if it were being managed better?

An advertising agency: "We've been taken by surprise too often. When our major customers cut ad budgets because of downturns and belt tightening in their industries, we would have information and budget-control systems in place that would allow us to cut costs quickly. Contingency marketing and sales programs would be in place so that slack resources could be quickly committed. We would stay closer to our customers in order to develop early warning systems."

- What would this opportunity look like if it were developed?

The respiratory-care unit of a hospital: "We would start a consultation and training service dealing with ventilator-dependent patients. Our clients would be other medical facilities dealing with this small but very expensive group. We would show how current technology could be used to discharge these patients safely either into a group home or into the care of relatives. The principal goal would be the improvement of the quality of life of these patients."

- What would exist that does not exist now?

An automobile manufacturer: "Our cars would be of a quality equal to or exceeding those of the Japanese. Our costs, which now run about 5 percent above our North American competitors, would be brought in line. We would make an industry breakthrough in terms of customer service."

- What kinds of risks would we be taking if we were a high flyer in our field?

A *high school*: "We would see our mission as service to the total community. Our programs would help our students integrate school with out-of-school experience, so that social-emotional development would go hand in hand with academic development. We would provide adults with opportunities to learn, develop, and participate in school activities."

- What kinds of decisions would we be implementing if we were moving forward?

  A *large manufacturer*: "We would be implementing a decision to close a plant that has long outlived its usefulness. However, we would like this to be a model plant closing. That is, the decision would be permeated by human values. First, we would like to work closely with the local community and part friends. Second, we would like to do whatever we could to care for the concerns of those who work there by offering transfers, early retirement packages, severance packages, outplacement counseling, and the like."

- You're looking at the company two years down the line, two *good* years. What do you see?

  The oldest and least efficient of five manufacturing facilities. The answer to this question is illustrated by Raab (1985) as he describes the design of a "future plant" outlined by a plant manager and his staff:

Their design featured a product group structure which would be managed utilizing a results focused, participative process. Operators would receive more information and be responsible for establishing and accomplishing performance goals. Supervisors would provide leadership through coordinating, coaching, and resourcing, rather than relying on their authority as "The Boss." Managers would utilize processes and systems supportive to those of supervisors and operators. Staffing would be set and managed within each product group. Based on increased trust, high commitment, and greater utilization of the workforce's abilities, a level of productivity and employee satisfaction comparable to the better new plants would exist. (p. 27)

Further stimulus questions, including questions tailored to specific cases, can be developed. Getting members of an organization to "future" enables *them* to discover discrepancies between what is and what could be. Brainstorming preferred scenarios produces lists of improvements rather than lists of things that are wrong.

The Advantages of Developing Preferred Scenarios

Locke and Latham (1984), in discussing goal setting, suggest by implication, four ways in which the development of preferred scenarios can help organizations:

• Developing preferred scenarios *focuses* the organization's *attention and action.* New scenarios give members a vision toward which they can direct their energies. Workers are less likely to engage in aimless behavior.

• Developing preferred scenarios *mobilizes* energy and effort. Members of organizations who seem lethargic during the problem exploration phase can come to life when alternate scenarios are spelled out. Developing scenarios is not just a cognitive exercise. Appealing scenarios drive action.

• Developing preferred scenarios *increases persistence.* Workers with a vision are not only energized to do something, but they tend to work harder and longer. Workers with clear and realistic agendas don't give up easily.

• Developing preferred scenarios *motivates* workers to search for *strategies* to accomplish them. That is, developing scenarios and agendas, a Stage-II task, leads naturally into a search for strategies and means, a Stage-III task.

EXAMPLE: Brainstorming by the performance planning and appraisal (PPA) task force at United International Airways leads to two major possibilities. The first would be to start with the reform of the current appraisal system, which is being used in only a perfunctory way. The new scenario would include a solid, timely review of each person's performance by both the person himself or herself and his or her manager or supervisor. The appraisal would also be reviewed by the supervisor's manager. Meaningful data would be entered on the appraisal forms and the forms would become part of the personnel record of each person. Finally, decisions such as job assignment, salary increases, and promotion would be based on the appraisals.

A second scenario would be to create and install a completely new comprehensive performance planning-feedback-appraisal system. In this scenario an effective appraisal system would be merely one part of the total three-part system. The new PPA system would start with collaborative objective setting between managers or supervisors and the people they manage. Individual plans would be based on organizational unit plans, and these in turn would be based on the strategic business plan of the organization. Next, managers would become responsible for developing a culture of feedback in their units. Self-feedback (the feedback each person gives himself or herself based on personal objectives and actual outcomes) and timely feedback from peers and supervisors would be designed into the system and become the norm. The incentives and rewards needed to make this a reality would be in place. Third, appraisals that would flow naturally from performance planning, and ongoing feedback would take place. Because of ongoing feedback, appraisals would not be surprises. Rather they would be opportunities to summarize and reinforce messages already delivered and to formalize decisions.

The appraisal meeting would be another opportunity for communication between managers or supervisors and staff. Mid-term appraisals would redirect individual performance plans, and yearly appraisals would pave the way for the next round of performance planning.

If the new PPA system is presented well, it will focus the organization's attention and action, it will mobilize energy and effort, it will increase persistence, and it will motivate the members of the organization to search for strategies to implement it.

ACTION IN STEP II-A

There is no reason to wait until the grand plan has been formulated to start getting some elements of a preferred scenario on line. As indicated above, a preferred scenario worth its salt mobilizes and focuses energy and suggests action steps.

> EXAMPLE: The new CEO of United International Airways presented a vision of a low-fare, low-cost airline. He stressed viability and flexibility in a deregulated world. The airline would offer service equal to that of the other giants, but would gain and maintain market share because of low fares in a wide variety of markets. Some of the best managers bought into this philosophy immediately and, knowing that the name of the game was going to be cost containment, began acting immediately. For instance, the new director of catering knew that he had to offer better meals but pay less for them. Since so little imagination had been used in catering, his task was not as difficult as it sounded. He began to experiment. He quickly discovered that the kind of meals that cost less were the ones that many passengers preferred. Many other managers followed the same line. They knew that UIA, as most organizations, had a fair amount of slack and fat left over from pre-deregulation days. This was especially true of one relatively high-cost airline that had been acquired recently.

Effective scenarios capture people's attention, provide motivation, and drive action. UIA went on to formulate strategies to bring costs into line, but the best and the brightest were already moving in that direction.

10

Step II-B:
Turning a Scenario
into a Viable Agenda

Once a range of future-scenario elements or possibilities has been brainstormed, they need to be evaluated for their relevance, specificity, realism, adequacy, fit with actual or proposed organizational culture (that is, assumptions, values, norms), and consequences. "What do we really need?" and "What is actually possible?" are the kinds of questions to be asked at this point. Figure 10-1 adds step II-B to the helping model. The goals of this step are:

A. To apply the principles by which preferred-scenario possibilities are turned into viable agenda.

B. To explore the consequences of the new-agenda outcomes.

C. To develop contingency scenarios in case anything prevents the preferred scenario from being implemented.

The purpose of separating the kind of critique called for in step II-B from the II-A process of imagining a better future is clear: Concomitant evaluation of options puts a damper on the use of imagination. Imagination needs to be unfettered for a while; otherwise, viable possibilities are overlooked.

We now return to one part of UIA's preferred scenario—a new, effective performance planning and appraisal system.

EXAMPLE: UIA believed that a mere reform of the appraisal system, no matter how professional, was an inadequate response to their needs. One of the problems was a *pro-forma* appraisal system not linked to organizational, unit, or individual planning. On the other hand, in-

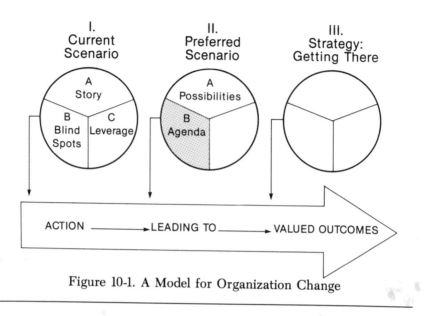

Figure 10-1. A Model for Organization Change

stalling a comprehensive PPA system seemed a very formidable task. Planning had been something relegated to the top of the organization. Planning at lower levels was a hit-and-miss affair. Furthermore, there was certainly no culture of feedback in the organization.

A comprehensive PPA system would put an enormous burden on managers, especially managers who had created an easy life for themselves. Still the new mission and strategic business plan demanded a total PPA system. Without such a system high-level plans could end up being just words, and the second state would be worse than the first. Managers would have to learn that PPA ultimately makes their jobs easier rather than more burdensome.

The task force studied other organizations and found that some had successfully installed comprehensive PPA systems under similar circumstances. Therefore it was possible. They interviewed managers who had at first resisted it but who later realized that they could not do without it. The members of the task force learned that the manner of installation was critical. They steeled themselves to the fact that new PPA systems often make the proverbial bloody entrance. It was also decided that a PPA system that would fit their own culture was needed. They rejected the idea of simply buying an off-the-shelf system.

This is an initial attempt to apply the principles by which a preferred scenario is turned into a viable agenda. It will also be necessary to explore the consequences of installing the new PPA system and to develop contingency plans in case anything prevents the PPA agenda from being implemented.

THE CRITERIA FOR FORMULATING
A VIABLE AGENDA

The word *agenda* here is taken in its root Latin sense, "that which is to be done," meaning that which is to be put in place in the company, institution, unit, or project. Visions, possibilities, images, and pictures create enthusiasm, but specific agendas drive behavior. In a sense, step II-A deals with creativity, while step II-B deals with innovation—bringing creative ideas on line. The preferred scenario needs to be appealing, but more than appealing. Here is a useful norm: Start with the future (vision, ideal, preferred scenario) and let yourself dream, *but* build an agenda that you will stake your job on. If the preferred scenario is complex, then it needs to be divided into its various parts, or each subunit must clearly understand which part of the larger agenda it is to pursue. Whether the preferred scenario is complex or simple, the following criteria are tools for turning a vision into a viable agenda. This shaping process means developing scenarios with the following characteristics:

1. Stated as accomplishments or outcomes rather than means or strategies.
2. Clear and specific.
3. Measurable or verifiable.
4. Realistic.
5. Substantive or at least adequate.
6. In keeping with the organization's overall strategy and values.
7. Set in a reasonable time frame.

These are the criteria used to determine whether the new scenario or any part of it is workable or not. These principles are tools for crafting an agenda. Each of these criteria will be briefly explored and illustrated.

1. State preferred scenarios in terms of outcomes or ac-complishments rather than programs or behavior leading up to these accomplishments. Preferred scenarios are not behaviors, but outcomes or accomplishments. They may, however, be *patterns* of behavior that need to be *in place.*

> EXAMPLE: Within the next year managers will have computerized all record keeping. They will be seeking out value-added ways of managing, including coaching.

It is a question of developing a past-participle approach (costs *reduced*, marketing skills *acquired and used*, a zero-defects program *implemented*, mid-year appraisal interviews *engaged in*) to scenario and agenda development. Stating new scenarios in terms of ac-complishments is not just a question of language. Outcomes need to be stated separately from the strategies or actions leading to their accomplishment.

2. State preferred scenarios in terms of clear, specific, and de-tailed outcomes. Scenarios stated, not only as outcomes, but as *specific* outcomes, tend to motivate or drive behavior.

> EXAMPLE: UIA will have a new hub-and-spoke system in place in St. Louis within one year from now. This hub will serve twenty dif-ferent destinations within eighteen months. The tentative list of cities to be served by this hub includes. . .

Vagueness is the bane of action. Grand language can be inspirational: "We will not only be an airline of excellence, but we will be one of the world's premier airlines." The clear and detailed delineation of specific outcomes provides direction and drives behavior. This is especially true if they are behaviors leading to service outcomes. It is fine to say, "We want satisfied customers," but what do satisfied customers look like in a variety of situations: when calling for a reser-vation, when eating a meal on a long flight, when checking bag-gage, when writing or calling with a complaint, when waiting for a delayed flight, and so forth?

3. **Develop scenarios in terms of outcomes that can be measured or verified.** Members of the organization must be able to tell whether or not they have achieved the outcomes for which they are responsible.

EXAMPLE: The CEO of an advertising agency called for "more effective teamwork" between the account executives and the creative people. How will he know when this goal is accomplished? First, he will know only if there is a behavioral definition of lack of teamwork; for instance, disagreements between the two, leading to increased time spent on projects and—in more serious cases—to loss of projects and even clients, when deadlines are missed. Second, he will know only if teamwork is defined in terms of behavioral patterns that actually contribute to both the timeliness and excellence of business outcomes.

Members of organizations cannot know whether they are making progress if they do not know where they started and precisely where they are going. It is not always necessary to count things in order to determine whether a goal has been reached, though sometimes counting is quite helpful. At any rate, one needs to be able to verify outcomes in some way.

4. **Make sure that the preferred scenario in its entirety and in its parts is realistic.** A scenario is realistic if (a) the resources necessary for its accomplishment are available, (b) internal and/or external obstacles do not prevent its accomplishment, (c) scenario outcomes are under the control of those responsible for them, and (d) the cost of bringing the new scenario on line is outweighed by the benefits it brings.

EXAMPLE: "Reduced costs" is part of UIA's preferred scenario. Being asked to cut costs does not bother most managers in UIA as much as being told how and where. Therefore, it was decided to leave the how and where of cost cutting to each manager. In some cases, where cost cutting involves the interactions between two departments, the how and where are left to joint decisions by the managers of the departments in question. As preparation for the cost-cutting venture, managers were asked to indicate what they would have to do to cut costs by 10, 15, and 20 percent and what the implications of each would be.

In this case managers retained control over outcomes and were not robbed of their autonomy. They became partners rather than adversaries in the cost-cutting venture.

EXAMPLE: Regarding the establishment of a new hub in St. Louis, it was determined that UIA either held or could acquire the requisite number of "slots," that the metropolitan work pool could provide enough skilled workers for the operation, that there was sufficient financing, and that the markets at the ends of the "spokes" in the hub-and-spokes operation warranted the expansion.

Goals should be set neither too high nor too low. If they are set too high, they can do more harm than good. Locke and Latham (1984) put it this way:

Nothing breeds success like success. Conversely, nothing causes feelings of despair like perpetual failure. A primary purpose of goal setting is to increase the motivation level of the individual. But goal setting can have precisely the opposite effect if it produces a yardstick that constantly makes the individual feel inadequate. (p. 39)

UIA must remember that cost-cutting practices to establish PPA systems are not just financial ventures. They are also social-emotional operations whose realism must be assessed from this persepctive.

   5. **Make sure that preferred scenarios are substantive, that they adequately address the problems to be managed and the opportunities to be developed.** Goals are unrealistic if they are too high, but they are inadequate if they are set too low. The research shows that, other things being equal, goals that make people stretch generally act as incentives. To be adequate, a set of outcomes envisioned must be relevant to the mission of the company or institution and contribute in some substantial way to managing the problem or opportunity in question. If the problem or opportunity is not clearly defined, then it may be impossible to determine whether any given scenario or goal is adequate.

EXAMPLE: A small airline in Chicago decided to change its marketing strategy. It decided to target business travelers almost exclusively. It changed its seating patterns to only two seats on each side of the aisle and provided other amenities liked by business travelers. In one way, the change was very successful. Business travelers loved the service. However, the airline did not fill enough seats to make a profit. The preferred scenario, turning the airline into an low-fare all-business operation, was inadequate. While it did generate a great deal of customer loyalty, it did not achieve the goal of increasing the number of seats filled.

"Will putting this new scenario in place get us where we want to go?" Unless the answer is "yes" or "probably yes" (within reasonable risk limits), changes in the agenda are called for.

6. Make sure that the preferred scenario is in keeping with the strategy and values of the organization. Step II-B asks two questions: "Are we doing the right thing in terms of our business?" and "Are we doing the right thing in terms of our philosophy and values?" The preferred scenario, if implemented, might well make the organization more profitable, but what other values might be ignored?

EXAMPLE: A conglomerate had the opportunity to buy a company with poor management. The company, however, did show promise. The conglomerate could take it over, install effective management, pump up its business, and sell it at a substantial profit within two years. However, the company in question was involved in a number of environmental disputes. It had been able, within existing laws, to keep environmentalists at bay, but it had angered many people. The conglomerate's managers would be able to keep environmentalists at bay during the two years they needed for the turnaround. But they decided not to buy it because they did not want to harm their image nor run the risk of violating their own values with respect to the environment.

When a company or institution establishes its mission, it is also time to identify and commit itself to the range of values which will guide its activities.

7. Make sure that there is a realistic time frame for putting the preferred scenario in place. Tasks that are to be accomplished "sometime or other" never seem to be achieved. Coming up with unrealistic time frames is also courting trouble. When things do not happen as quickly as they are supposed to, members of the organization and other stakeholders—such as banks and investors—can become dispirited.

> EXAMPLE: A computer company, in order to retain current customers and increase market share, announced the introduction of a range of attractive products and a new, steamlined service program. This drew the attention of both customers and the media. However, the introduction of the new products fell behind the announced schedule. Customers, both current and prospective, began turning to other products. And the new service system needed to be rethought before it could be introduced. Even customers who had not been dissatisfied with the previous service program began to grumble.

As we shall see in step III-C, plans are ways of making time an ally instead of an enemy.

A new scenario, to be a workable package of outcomes, must meet all the above requirements. If one is missing, it may prove to be the fatal flaw in the movement toward problem-managing or opportunity-developing action.

ACTION IN STEP II-B

Some people, when introduced to a challenging vision of the future, act immediately in a variety of ways to move the vision toward reality. For them, vision drives action. Others are moved to act once the vision is translated into the kind of detail suggested here. The vision catches their imaginations, but specificity drives action.

> EXAMPLE: The director of catering at UIA announced the new policy of higher-quality and lower-cost meals. He called together his troops and spelled out what this would mean. For instance, nutritious snacks, which cost less and fit the needs of many passengers more, would be substituted as often as possible for full meals. Once some of his managers got the more detailed picture, they launched immediately into action. For instance, one quickly did a review of the catering services of other airlines and studied those that had moved toward using snacks more frequently. Another chose one route and began to experiment with a variety of lighter meals immediately. He soon gathered very useful data on the reactions of passengers.

Again, people do not need to wait for the grand plan to be announced. Leaping into action, if the actions are reasonable and outcome-oriented, is a sign of organizational health.

WEIGHING THE CONSEQUENCES OF PUTTING A PREFERRED SCENARIO IN PLACE

As March (1982) notes, decision making as a rational process requires a knowledge of alternatives (the possible scenarios), a knowledge of the consequences of each alternative, a consistent preference ordering (for instance, business outcomes over mere organizational outcomes), and a decision rule—for instance, "Select the alternative that will maximize the expected value" (p. 30). Therefore, if organizations are to make reasonable decisions about preferred scenarios, they need to explore the consequences of their preferences. Just because a scenario *can* be implemented does not mean that it is *wise* to implement it. The following are kinds of questions that can be asked:

- What impact will this scenario have on business outcomes in the short term? in the long term?

- What impact will this scenario have on quality of work life in the short term? in the long term?

- What will the costs and benefits be to key stakeholders in the short term? in the long term?

EXAMPLE: Since UIA wanted to be a low-fare, low-cost airline, it studied the possible consequences of this scenario by examining the experience of a similar airline it recently acquired. That airline was a "no-frills" operation. They charged for meals and handling baggage, overbooked their flights, and skimped on their reservations system. The consequences were harried employees, unanswered phones, disgruntled passengers, and the inability to attract business travelers. Since none of these consequences were acceptable to UIA, it was necessary to revisit the preferred scenario in order to make sure that its various parts would not lead to these consequences.

It goes without saying that the decision-making process is not always as rational as March suggests. For instance, long-term consequences are often overlooked. Businesses in the United States are currently being faulted for consistently taking a short-term economic outlook. Some say that such short-term perspectives are no longer feasible as we move even more rapidly from a national to a world economy.

DEVELOPING CONTINGENCY SCENARIOS

It is impossible to predict all events that might affect the implementation of a preferred scenario. This is especially true if the environment is turbulent. One reason for brainstorming a range of scenario possibilities is to develop a set of fall-back positions in case some unexpected events prevent the implementation of a scenario or some part of it.

> EXAMPLE: The airline that wanted to be an all-business carrier had developed a back-up position: two-tier service like other airlines. It would remain a low-fare alternative to the bigger airlines in certain markets. It would slowly move into other markets as warranted by the business climate. It had no intention of growing too quickly and forcing showdowns with larger carriers.
>
> There was one event, however, that it had not counted on. The city in which it was based had two airports, and it was based, unobtrusively, at the much smaller airport. A much bigger low-fare airline, which used the larger airport, decided to move some of its flights to the smaller in order to compete better with the full-cost airlines. One full-cost airline announced that it, too, was moving some of its flights to the smaller airport. Both larger airlines would be serving some of the same cities as the smaller. Now what?

Now what, indeed? It was probably unrealistic for the smaller airline to assume that the "big guys" were going to stay away forever, but it did not expect competition to arrive so quickly. In developing preferred scenarios in turbulent environments, it is essential to ask, "What can *possibly* happen that will upset the applecart? How can this scenario go wrong?" Asking these questions is not indulging in pessimism, but realism.

11

Step II-C:
Commitment—Linking
the Agenda to Action

There comes a time when the sponsors of a change project need to say: "This is the scenario we want, it's realistic, and we're going to implement it." This kind of commitment may or may not be implied in the decision to start the entire change process and in the work that is done up to this point, but sometimes commitment to a preferred scenario needs to be done formally. Figure 11-1 adds this choice-and-commitment step to Stage II.

Target groups must see that sponsors of the change project are serious and are willing to commit themselves and resources to the agenda. Half-hearted commitment on the part of managers and other sponsors ("It would be good for the institution if this project were to be completed, so why don't you see what you can do about it?") provides little incentive for hard work and risk taking on the part of the staff. Commitment is one of those nice, warm words. It needs to be demythologized. We know it is present only when members of the organization engage in actions that lead to the accomplishment of the change agenda. At this point three questions can be asked: How should the change agenda be communicated to the members of the organization? What strategies can be used to gain commitment? How can a climate of learning be built around the agenda?

COMMUNICATING THE AGENDA

Since organizations are social systems, the link between agenda and action is not just technical, that is, a question of strategies and plans;

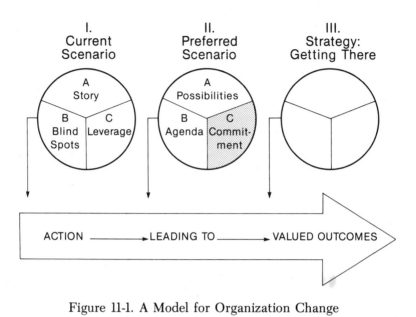

Figure 11-1. A Model for Organization Change

it is also social-emotional. Therefore, the way in which the agenda is communicated to those responsible for its implementation is crucial. As we have seen in Model A, leaders communicate their agendas in ways that arouse enthusiasm. The ideal is that people rally 'round the agenda.

EXAMPLE: In one organization the task forces responsible for restructuring the organization at the service of its business asked themselves, "How much shall we tell the other members of the organization as we move along with our work?" One possibility was to finish the job and merely announce the new agenda. This was possible since the organization was patriarchal and had a culture of compliance and obedience. However, it was evident that it was this precise culture that robbed the organization of the kind of creativity and risk taking needed in its business. Therefore, they established a newsletter that kept people informed of their progress and gave people an opportunity to contribute to and challenge their work. They wanted as many people as possible on board from the moment the preferred scenario was announced. To achieve this, they needed the participation of staff throughout the entire process.

Communicating the agenda is a *process* that begins well before the agenda is put into its final form.

In major change projects the leader of the company or institution should present the agenda, at least in its broad outline. The advantages of the new agenda should be pointed out together with an honest appraisal of some of the difficulties the organization faces in implementing the agenda.

> EXAMPLE: After divestiture from AT&T, one Bell Telephone executive said something like this: "We are entering a New Age, an age of economic turbulence and world-wide competition. In the old Bell people were rewarded for compliance and for staying within the limits of their jobs. In the new Bell we need a new ethic: Every person a problem solver, every worker a salesperson. We need to be patient with one another as we implement this new ethic, but we must all move as quickly as the new economic world we live in demands."

The way in which an agenda is presented can help forge the link between vision and action.

As mentioned in Model A, leadership is needed at all levels of the organization. Therefore, the new agenda needs to be communicated by leaders all the way down the line. Many agendas lose the name of action because they are not taken by each leader down the line and tailored to the role of each unit. If Bell wants a culture of problem solving, then all managers and supervisors must, each in his or her own way, announce this agenda to their units and keep announcing it by modeling the kinds of behavior that support it.

STRATEGIES FOR GAINING COMMITMENT

In some organizations the sponsors of change projects hope that people will commit themselves to the preferred scenarios that have been formulated, but they do little to promote buy-in. On the assumption that commitment is not an automatic process, the search for strategies to promote commitment is important. In general, this means a search for the kinds of *incentives* that make sense for *these* people, in *this* organization, at *this* time, with respect to *this* agenda, under *these* conditions. Incentives are not incentives unless they are perceived as such by the actors in question. Here are some suggestions.

- **Participation.** Encourage people to participate in the formulation of the change agenda. Ownership of the preferred scenario is a process that begins, ideally, with the beginning of the change process in step I-A. Participation does not mean decision by consensus. It can be as simple as giving people an opportunity to have their say. For instance, early on everyone in UIA was given a check list of business and organizational problems and of principles of excellence. They were asked to check whichever ones they felt pertained to the airline.

- **Appealing Agendas.** Agendas that are substantive and appealing in themselves create enthusiasm. People identify readily with substantive causes even when they are challenging. When UIA's CEO says, "We're going to do what the so-called experts say can't be done—build a large low-fare, low-cost airline that serves its customers well and is tough enough to survive the turbulence of a deregulated industry," it's the kind of message that can hit home to those for whom challenges are incentives.

- **Detailed Agendas.** As suggested earlier, clear, specific agendas drive behavior. The details need not be technical; they can be stated as facts or spelled out in pictures, stories, or whatever. Details help people get a feeling for the realism of the agenda. They can see it, touch it, taste it. In UIA the director of catering called his team together and said, "Here's what catering in this airline is going to look like," and then spelled out the preferred scenario in terms of contrasting pictures. "On the Chicago to Washington run, morning travelers have had to look at cheese omelets and blackened sausages floating in grease for years. No more. Light fares—bagels, instant hot cereals, fresh fruit, granola, and the like. We're jumping on the nutrition bandwagon for passengers who want nutrition."

- **Emotions.** Effective communicators can highlight the emotional appeal of the agenda. If workers are hurting, they point out ways in which the agenda offers hope and relief. If they are in bondage, ways in which the new agenda will be liberating can be highlighted. For instance, in UIA a new agenda sparked off enthusiasm in the marketing department where people felt that their ability to exercise creativity had been thwarted. They came up with a ticket-giveaway venture that drew fifty thousand people to a stadium and gave the airline free press across the entire country.

• **Flexible Agendas.** Agendas with options, agendas that can be tailored to the needs of different organizational units, are appealing. For instance, in announcing the new performance planning and appraisal system, UIA management stressed the objectives of the system and outlined a general framework to achieve these objectives. But each unit, while not free to do without a PPA system, was given the opportunity to tailor the framework to its own needs. Those working in each unit were given a say about the format. As a result, it was *their* PPA system, not one forced on them by management or, even worse, by the personnel department. *cf. Order fate's process – mandated by H.R.*

• **Resources.** The realism and therefore the appeal of an agenda is heightened if it includes a promise of resources to implement it. For instance, even in the face of severe cost cutting, the marketing department of UIA was given an increased budget and allowed to hire a few highly creative people. Its mandate was simple: Fill seats. With respect to the PPA system, personnel offered consulting services to any unit wanting help in tailoring the PPA framework to its own needs. Workshops were set up for managers and supervisors, but attendance was not mandatory. Even individual workers could request help in formulating their priorities and objectives.

• **Modeling at the Top.** Leaders model the behaviors they want to put in place in the organization. The announcement of the PPA program at UIA included a statement from the CEO of the new mission and strategy for the airline plus the performance objectives that he, in consultation with senior managers and the board, was setting for himself. He instructed the vice presidents to follow the same procedure and to see to it that their senior managers followed the same process until the PPA system cascaded throughout the airline. The performance objectives of every manager were to be public within his or her own unit.

• **Projects.** Get people active around some part of the preferred agenda early on. Salt the institution with pilot projects. This keeps attention focused on the agenda. For instance, a university, as part of its new mission, wanted to encourage interdisciplinary institutes and projects. Since the culture of the institution supported segmentalism among the academic disciplines, the sponsors moved slowly. Small interdisciplinary conferences were held. For instance, a conference on AIDS was jointly sponsored by psychology, sociology, and pastoral studies. These events proved to be very successful. A master's program in organizational studies was established with a very small core faculty. It reported directly to the graduate school but drew adjunct faculty from psychology, sociology, education, and anthropology. More and more people began to notice and become involved in these interdisciplinary ventures.

ESTABLISHING A CLIMATE
OF LEARNING AND PROBLEM SOLVING

As suggested in Model A, leaders not only communicate their system-enhancing agendas in ways that arouse interest and enthusiasm, but they also build a climate of learning and problem solving around these agendas. This means that the agenda is so presented that it stimulates those involved with it to engage in the kind of learning, innovation, and problem solving that will serve the agenda. For instance, the director of management development for a large organization outlined such a compelling management-development program that it stimulated others outside his unit to contribute to it. Managers who had attended programs outside the company sent him copies of their programs. Others sent him articles they had read in various magazines and journals.

> EXAMPLE: In UIA the fill-seats agenda of the marketing department aroused a great deal of enthusiasm. A task force was established to discover and review every successful trick that any airline in the world had used over the past fifteen years to attract passengers. These constituted a data base for piggy-back brainstorming. Ideas that had worked ten years before but which had become outdated were transformed into current ideas. For instance, a sleepy advertisement encouraging people to "give yourself a quick break" and a market report in *Forbes* ("The Vanishing Vacation," 1986)—which indicated that the traditional two-week domestic holiday is changing in many markets, giving way to shorter, more frequent, and less expensive

trips—were tied together in a National Getaway Weekend promotion. The airline itself declared one January weekend "National Getaway Weekend." It proved so successful that a similar promotion was mounted for each of the seasons of the year.

ACTION IN STEP II-C

Step II-C is also a stimulus and channel for agenda-promoting action. For instance, if people are promised the resources needed to promote an agenda, this may well move them to act even before the grand plan is in place.

EXAMPLE: When a city announced that it would begin to move toward a total office-automation system in order to provide better service at a reduced cost, the people in the department of streets and sanitation knew that it would be some time before the computer terminals actually sat on their desks. The director talked to a computer whiz who worked in the department and to the principal of a nearby high school, which had dozens of computers that were idle after school and on weekends. An arrangement was made whereby the department was given access to the computers when they were not being used for school purposes. A few of them were actually moved to the department, and selected upper-class students were allowed to come and see computers in action. It was a win-win arrangement. Since so much time was saved by using the computers, the departmental computer whiz became an internal consultant to their use. She also knew that the data generated could be transferred to the department's computers when they eventually came on line.

In this case, informal actions constituted a sign of commitment and prepared the way for the formal implementation process.

STAGE III

GETTING THERE:
STRATEGIES AND PLANS

Overview

Strategies for Getting There

Choosing Strategies

Formulating Plans

12

An Overview of Stage III

While Stage II deals with *what* needs to be accomplished or put in place, Stage III deals with *how* that is to be accomplished in terms of strategies and plans. It is absolutely essential to remember, however, that developing strategies and plans for moving the current scenario to the preferred scenario is still a cognitive exercise. Strategies for action are not to be confused with outcome-producing action itself. The excitement of coming up with innovative action strategies is beguiling. However, these strategies—regardless of how innovative they are—need to be implemented and are subject to both inertia and entropy.

The three steps of Stage III are:

A. Brainstorming strategies for moving from the current to the preferred scenario.

B. Choosing the best-fit package of strategies for each outcome.

C. Turning these strategies into a viable plan.

In complex change programs, strategies need to be elaborated for each outcome of the preferred scenario.

A. Brainstorm a wide range of strategies to accomplish each new-scenario outcome. Imagination is absolutely essential here. The temptation is to think of one or two strategies and then move immediately to action. In some cases this is fine. Common sense makes it clear that the chosen strategy is going to do the job. In many cases, however, the failure to brainstorm a range of strategies leads to either ineffectiveness (the chosen strategy does not work) or inefficiency (a different strategy would have accomplished the outcome at a lower cost). In practice, some people—once they know where they are headed—instinctly choose the right way to get there. But sometimes instincts are wrong, as the following example indicates.

> EXAMPLE: A large chemical company recently instituted an early retirement scheme to trim down the organization. However, more than twice the anticipated number of employees took advantage of the scheme. The result? The company had to hire back many of the retirees as consultants at hefty salaries.

The lesson is clear: Beware of the single-strategy approach to change.

B. Choose the best-fit strategy or package of strategies for each new-scenario outcome. Brainstorming a range of strategies is a double-edged sword. On the one hand, it can lead to greater productivity. On the other, it can leave members of the organization in a quandary with respect to which strategy or set of strategies to use.

> EXAMPLE: An intriguing example of a possible mischoice of strategies is reported by Gary Burtless of the Brookings Institution (see "How Benefits Can Backfire," 1986). The Federal government gives tax credits to employers who hire "disadvantaged" workers. The desired outcome is clear—increased employment of the disadvantaged. But there is evidence that some employers pass up the tax incentives because they are afraid to hire people the program brands as disadvantaged. If this is the case, then the strategy has, at least for some, an effect opposite to the one intended. Burtless believes that the money would be better spent if it were used to train the disadvantaged.

Step III-A calls for a range of strategies; step III-B calls for the right choice of strategies. The right choice is difficult without a range from which to choose.

C. Cast the strategy or set of strategies into the form of a viable plan. Plans tell us such things as *what* needs to be done, the *order* in which things need to be done, *who* is to do what, and who needs to *coordinate* the entire process. Plans are ways of making time a friend instead of an enemy. All the work of Model A will be fruitless if, ultimately, someone ultimately has to say, "The preferred scenario was good and the strategies we chose to implement it were excellent, but we ran out of time."

EXAMPLE: One problem with North American automobile manufacturers is the time lag between the identification of needed changes and the implementation of these changes. Automobile redesign can take years. The computer industry does not want to fall into the same trap. A small computer company wanted to design a range of computers around a new, sophisticated high-speed chip. They knew that speed in bringing the new products to market would make a huge difference. They took advantage of the latest and most comprehensive project-management software available. As soon as breakthroughs in design were achieved, they could immediately use the project-management program to reorder subsequent steps in their overall project plan. They also made sure that marketing efforts were integrated with project development.

As a result, they designed the new line of computers and brought them to market in record time. Since the work of the marketing group was completely integrated with the work of both R&D and manufacturing, the machines were actually available two weeks before they were promised. Industry analysts gave high marks not only to the machines, but also to the company: "It delivers on its promises and delivers on time" was free advertising and music to the ears of those who had worked the plan.

In complex projects, complex plans need to be divided into subparts, but the integration of the subparts needs to be monitored constantly. In another computer company, marketing plans were not integrated with those of manufacturing. Their new lap-top computer was ready, but no one knew about it. When people called the company, it was almost impossible to find anyone who could answer questions about it.

Another way of looking at Stage III is to see it as the *engineering* stage of change. How do we engineer our way from the current to the preferred scenario? What details must be managed in the transition from where we are to where we want to be? The three steps spell out the engineering details.

13

Step III-A:
Strategies for Getting There

The world is constantly looking for more effective and efficient ways of moving to preferred scenarios and implementing goals. Consider the following situations and the questions they create.

• In many parts of the country, company-service industries are struggling to fill their entry-level jobs (see Nasar, 1986). The supply of workers is shrinking even as demand rises. What strategies can be used to attract workers into these jobs?

• The Internal Revenue Service realizes that there is a huge underground economy that remains untaxed (see Murray, 1986). Taxing this economy would help reduce the deficit. Are there more clever strategies for catching cheaters than the ones currently in use? Or are there other ways of taxing the underground economy?

• A chemical company, because of a downturn in the economy and increased competition, needs to trim down. What strategies can be used to reduce its work force by 10 percent?

• In the early Eighties both labor and management realized that health costs were getting out of control (see Bernstein, 1986). They joined forces in asking, "What can to be done to control skyrocketing health costs?" Here are some of the strategies they have been using:

1. Requiring members to get second opinions before surgery.

2. Encouraging workers to audit and challenge hospital and doctor bills.

3. Having workers get tests before being admitted to the hospital.

4. Setting up boards to determine whether hospitalization is necessary.

5. Having boards determine how long a hospital stay should be.

6. Providing incentives for outpatient surgery.

7. Monitoring the history of treatments to make sure they are needed.

8. Cross-checking insurance policies to make sure the same bill is not being paid by different carriers.

Experts claim that there is a way to go in cutting costs without cutting benefits, but the above strategies have been paying off. For instance, the cost that General Motors' health plan added to the price of a car dropped from $400 to about $360.

> EXAMPLE: Establishing a preferred scenario and then taking the time to brainstorm strategies for putting it in place are directly opposed to the "Well, this hasn't worked, so let's try something else" approach. Yet, an amazing number of individuals and organizations are still addicted to this outdated trial-and-error approach. One reason it is still in favor is that it is action-oriented: "Here's a possible solution; let's try it and see what happens."

CREATIVITY AND THE DEVELOPMENT OF STRATEGIES

Strategy is the art of identifying and choosing realistic means for achieving goals or objectives and doing so under adverse (for example, wartime) conditions. The problem situations in which companies and institutions are immersed constitute adverse conditions; they often are at war with themselves or with the turbulent environments around them. Figure 13-1 adds step III-A to Model B.

Once agendas are established, getting them accomplished is not just a matter of hard work. The research on problem solving (D'Zurilla and Goldfried, 1971; Heppner, 1978) suggests that the quality and efficacy of strategies tends to be better if they are chosen from among a number of possibilities. Therefore, developing strategies is an exercise in creativity. A review of the requirements

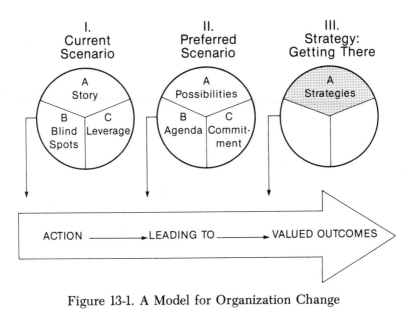

I.
Current
Scenario

A
Story

B
Blind
Spots

C
Leverage

II.
Preferred
Scenario

A
Possibilities

B
Agenda

C
Commit-
ment

III.
Strategy:
Getting There

A
Strategies

ACTION ———————►LEADING TO————————► VALUED OUTCOMES

Figure 13-1. A Model for Organization Change

for creativity (Cole & Sarnoff, 1980; Robertshaw, Mecca, & Rerick, 1978) shows that people often fail to use whatever creative resources they might have, especially in crisis situations. The creative person or organization is characterized by: optimism and confidence, acceptance of ambiguity and uncertainty, a wide range of interests, flexibility, tolerance for complexity, verbal fluency, curiosity, drive and persistence, independence, and nonconformity or reasonable risk taking. On the other hand, innovation is hindered by such things as fear, fixed habits, dependence on authority, and perfectionism. Again these may be individual or organizational problems. Some organizations have cultures that stimulate creativity; others have cultures that inhibit it.

BRAINSTORMING

One excellent way of surfacing possible strategies and tactics for moving from the current to the preferred scenario is brainstorming. Brainstorming is a technique for generating ideas, possibilities, or alternate courses of action. The brainstormer tries, through divergent thinking, to identify as many ways of achieving a goal as possible. There are certain rules that help make this technique work: suspending judgment, eliminating normal constraints to thinking, producing as many ideas as possible, using one idea as a takeoff for others, and producing even more ideas by clarifying items on the list.

Suspending Judgment

Suspending judgment means not criticizing the strategies being generated. This is one way of handling the tendency on the part of some to play a yes-but game. This rule forbids comments such as "Yes, but how would that work?"; "I like that idea, but"; "Your suggestion might actually work, but"; or even "You'd better explain what you mean"; or "I'm not sure about that idea." In one mid-sized organization tortured by a culture of perfectionism, the managers in a course on creative problem solving found it almost impossible to brainstorm strategies. They kept breaking the rule about criticizing options. Even when a trainer was placed in the group to challenge violations of the brainstorming rules, the participants said that they criticized the suggestions mentally—even their own suggestions!

Eliminating Normal Constraints

Eliminating normal constraints means letting yourself go. Include even wild possibilities. Later on it is easier to cut suggested strategies down to size than to expand them. The wildest possibilities often have within them at least a kernel of an idea that will work. People often need "permission" to let themselves go, even in such a harmless way. *PS News* (1982) put it this way:

> Too often we repress "good" ideas because when they are first stated they sound foolish. The idea is to create an atmosphere where such apparently foolish ideas will not only be accepted but encouraged. (p. 14)

Think of conservative strategies, liberal strategies, radical strategies, and even outrageous strategies.

Encouraging Quantity

Research on brainstorming shows that quantity generates quality. Develop as many alternates as possible. This increases the possibility of finding useful strategies. Studies show that some of the best ideas come along later in the brainstorming process. Some say that the quantity principle is the central one in strategy development (D'Zurilla & Nezu, 1980).

Piggybacking

Without criticizing any of the proposals, add on to strategies already generated and combine different ideas to form new possibilities. Variations and new twists in strategies already identified are taken as new ideas. For instance, when someone in UIA suggested an employee assistance plan to improve quality of work life, someone else suggested a self-help counseling service for flight attendants, and a third suggested a physical- and mental-health newsletter designed specifically for airline personnel and the kinds of problems and stress they face. Here one idea sparked the next, but the second idea did not negate nor replace the previous one.

Clarifying Items

Without criticizing suggestions, participants can ask for clarification. When a proposal is clarified, it can be expanded. Clarifying ideas often leads to new possibilities. The danger here, of course, is that people will use requests for clarification as a more subtle way of criticizing others' suggestions.

Brainstorming is not the same as free association. While workers are encouraged to think of even wild possibilities, still these possibilities must in some way be stimulated by and relate to the organizational problem or opportunity and the preferred agenda. Therefore, brainstorming itself is influenced by the way in which the problem or opportunity has been defined and the clarity and concreteness of the preferred scenario. Concreteness is as important in this strategy-development step as it is in the problem-clarification and agenda-setting stages.

AN EXAMPLE OF BRAINSTORMING

Many organizations, including United International Airways, are currently downsizing. Some of the larger companies are setting up outplacement units in their personnel departments, while others are hiring outplacement firms, a business that is booming (Machan, 1987). The preferred scenario is that those being let go find compatible jobs, at a equitable salary, within a reasonable time frame. The outplacement firms say that it currently takes the average person about 3.2 months to find work, but that the majority secure equivalent or better-paying positions. Of course, those are the figures for nonrecession times.

Feingold (1979) has compiled a list of job-hunting strategies that UIA's new outplacement unit finds useful. All things being equal, the more job-seeking techniques used, the better a person's chances of finding a compatible position.

The following strategies are the fruit of brainstorming. They are not listed in any particular order (Feingold, 1979, pp. 14-15)[1].

1. Newspaper: Place or answer an ad in a periodical.
2. Magazine: Place or answer an ad in a periodical.
3. Read the *Professional Trade Association Job Finder* (Garrett Park Press, Garrett Park, Maryland 20896).
4. Job banks: Use services that list candidates for jobs.
5. Job registries: This is another form of job bank.
6. Clearinghouse of jobs: Use employment services that list candidates and vacancies.
7. Clearinghouse of jobs: Use employment services set up in conjunction with national or regional meetings of professional organizations.
8. Cold canvass in person: Call on employers in the hope of finding a vacancy appropriate for your skills, personality, and interests.
9. Cold canvass by telephone: Call employers to identify organizations with appropriate vacancies.
10. Union hiring hall: Use employment services set up by labor organizations.
11. Alumni office contacts: School or college alumni offices may suggest the names of former students who are in a position to help you.
12. Public career-counseling services: Use state employment and other public career-oriented services.

---

[1]From "Merging Careers: Occupations for Post-Industrial Society" by S. N. Feingold, 1984, *The Futurist*, 18(1), 9-16. Copyright 1984. Reprinted by permission.

13. Private career and counseling services: The fees charged by these organizations may be more than justified by the job-search time saved.

14. Employment agencies: These may charge a fee or a percentage commission—but only if you take a job through them.

15. Executive search firms: These are "headhunter" organizations retained by employers to identify persons for specialized jobs.

16. Volunteer work: Millions have begun their career by first gaining experience and thus a foot in the door through unpaid work.

17. Part-time work experience: A part-time job may be easier to obtain than full-time work and may lead to a permanent position.

18. Temporary or summer work: These provide experience and an introduction to the employer's organization.

19. Make your own job: Freelance work may lead to self-employment or to a job with an employer.

20. Join a 40-plus group: Most cities have these job clubs that specialize in older workers.

21. Join a 65-plus group: These organizations provide jobs and other services for senior citizens.

22. Join a job-search group: Sharing job-hunting experiences can provide new ideas and psychological support.

23. Tell friends and acquaintances: Studies show that friends and family are the best single source of job leads.

24. Federal job centers: These offices, located in major cities, are a good source of job leads. Look them up in the telephone book under "U.S. Government."

25. Computerized placement services: Many organizations inventory candidates and employers by computers to make job matches.

26. Social-agency placement services: Along with social services, many of these groups now provide job counseling and placement assistance.

27. Membership services: Many professional and other organizations maintain employment-assistance programs to aid their members.

28. Mail-order job campaign: Send out dozens or hundreds of letters to potential employers, hoping to identify suitable openings.

29. School or college placement services: Both current students and alumni generally are eligible for help from these groups.

30. Association placement services: Many professional and other organizations include employment assistance as part of their service programs.

31. Trade placement services: In many occupations, an organized placement program operates.

32. Professional placement services: Use professional career-placement specialists, particularly if looking for a high-level job.

33. Hotlines: Use these answering services (many operate twenty-four hours a day) maintained by community organizations or libraries.

34. Federal Civil Service offices: Contact employment offices of Federal agencies in your area of interest.

35. State merit service offices: Get in touch with appropriate state government agencies.

36. County or city personnel office: File for suitable openings with agencies of local government.

37. Internships: Use a paid or unpaid short-term internship to gain experience and make contact with potential employers.

38. Work-study programs: Use a cooperative work-study program to gain experience and to make contacts in a field of prime interest.

39. Networking: Expand contacts that may help you by working with peers, friends, supervisors, and others.

40. Mentor: Cultivate an older, more experienced person to whom you can turn for advice. Such a mentor may take a special interest in your proper placement.

41. Television job and career announcements: Don't overlook ads placed on television for employees.

42. Radio job and career announcement: Many employers, with numerous jobs, use radio to help solicit candidates for them.

43. Bulletin-board posting: Check ads placed on career-related bulletin boards.

44. Check the *College Placement Annual*, published by the College Placement Council (P.O. Box 2263, Bethlehem, PA 18001).

45. Check in-house job vacancies: Most progressive employers now post all vacancies for their current employees to examine and, if interested, apply for.

46. DVR job-placement services: All state divisions of rehabilitation services offer disabled persons extensive job counseling and placement services.

47. Former employers: Don't hesitate to ask former employers for help.

48. Fellow employees: Persons who work with you might know of suitable vacancies in other offices or organizations.

49. Personnel-office counseling: Many times, the personnel office will counsel you about career paths or alternative jobs in your organization.

50. Religious leaders: Often ministers, rabbis, and priests know of potential employers among their members.

51. Library resources: Check *Moody's Industrials*, the *Fortune* "500" list, and other library reference books for employment suggestions.

52. Overseas work: Major religious groups and other international agencies may hire for jobs in other countries.

53. Sponsored interviews: If possible, have persons you know set up employment contacts for you.

54. Military services: Enlistment in one of the armed services may provide both an immediate salary and job training in fields of interest.

Members of UIA's outplacement unit use this list as a starting point and expand it by their own brainstorming and by brainstorming with those looking for new jobs. This list illustrates the point that in brainstorming, quantity precedes quality. The very length of the list makes it clear that some of the best strategies for pursuing both business and organizational agendas are never identified because organizational players cut the brainstorming process too short.

EXAMPLE: Brainstorming strategies for installing the new performance planning and appraisal system in UIA was essential to both effectiveness and commitment. The PPA implementation task force at UIA wanted to come up with a plan that would reduce and manage expected resistance while still delivering PPA outcomes. A list of possible strategies included the following:

- Present unit managers with a flexible PPA format that they can adapt to their units through consultation with their staff.
- Introduce the PPA system gradually. Starting at the top, cascade it through the organization.
- Keep everyone informed about each implementation step.
- Get the CEO and his vice presidents to do PPA first. Let everyone know that this is a tool for every manager.
- Make the *manager* or *supervisor* of each unit, including the CEO and the vice presidents, the PPA project director for his or her unit.
- Do not hand PPA over to the personnel department for implementation. Train personnel managers and officers to become consultants to managers.
- Train managers and supervisors in the essentials of the PPA system. Train them so that they are capable of helping their staff understand and implement the system.
- Use outside trainers rather than the personnel department to prevent people from seeing PPA as a personnel project rather than a managerial initiative.
- Help people see that they already know and do much of what is required by an effective PPA system, for instance, setting objectives and drawing up work programs.
- Before starting PPA, make sure that all employees understand the mission of UIA, the mission of their own units, and how their mission relates to the mission of the larger unit of which it is a part.

Since the installation of PPA is such a substantial undertaking in a large organization, brainstorming strategies relating to each phase of the implementation process would be wise—preparation strategies, strategies for introducing performance planning, strategies for the development of a culture of ongoing feedback, and strategies for the introduction of an appraisal system. At each stage, then, there would be a pool of strategies from which the best could be chosen.

ACTION IN STEP III-A

The action strategies generated in step III-A do not constitute action itself, but they can be powerful incentives to action. Brainstorming is liberating. The alternatives generated empower people to act without the need to wait for the grand plan. In a mental-health center, the professional staff, discouraged by the fact that those in the community most in need of help were precisely those most difficult to reach, brainstormed a range of ways of making contact with these people. Suggestions included "helping by wandering around the neighborhood" and a whole host of other stimulating ideas. They met formally again two weeks after the brainstorming session. They discovered that over two-thirds of the group tried one or more of the strategies that had been brainstormed without waiting for the center to formulate and adopt new outreach programs. However, their experiences proved invaluable in formulating these programs.

Action itself generates action strategies. For instance, the value of pilot projects does not lie entirely in determining whether or not a course of action is feasible and effective. The very implementation of a program, even when it is only partially successful or actually fails, can suggest all sorts of strategies for making it successful.

EXAMPLE: The marketing department of UIA decided to use the Chicago-Denver route to test a variety of programs. It tried some innovative ski-package programs which proved to be only moderately successful in that highly competitive market. However, as spring and summer approached, it realized two things: first, for many the Rockies mean snow and skiing; second, many, many more do not ski. The mediocre success in the pilot ski-package programs stimulated the design of a marketing program that said, more or less, "Nonskiers take heart; the Rockies are finally yours." This program worked so well that the next winter a program was aimed directly at the nonskier; it said, "Hate skiing, but love the Rockies in winter." It described a dozen different ways in which the Rockies could be enjoyed by the nonskier.

The kinds of informal action proposed here and in the steps reviewed up to this point do not constitute a hit-or-miss approach to problem solving and change. Rather, relevant outcome-producing action is always welcome. All steps in Model B need to be seen as triggers and channels for action.

14

Step III-B:
Choosing Strategies

Once a range of possible strategies has been identified, change agents need to choose those that provide the best fit, that is, strategies that are most effective and efficient in both the long and short run. It is useless to have organizational players brainstorm strategies if they are unable to choose the best. Figure 14-1 adds step III-B to Model.

Although having a large number of possible strategies can be a problem in its own right because participants then have a hard time picking the best, having too few to choose from, as in the case of the chemical company that instituted an early-retirement plan

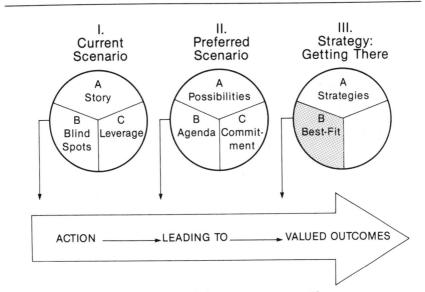

Figure 14-1. A Model for Organization Change

(mentioned in the introduction to Stage III), can be an even greater problem.

CHOOSING BEST-FIT STRATEGIES

Since III-B is a decision-making step, criteria are essential. The criteria for choosing strategies are similar to those for choosing a preferred scenario.

• **Choose a strategy or a set of strategies from a pool of strategies.** Both effectiveness and efficiency can be impaired if an organization chooses the first strategy that comes to mind: "The organization needs to be trimmed; therefore, search out nonperformers and fire them." Not only might such a strategy have consequences that will seriously disrupt the change effort, but there might be other strategies or a package of strategies that will accomplish the goal much more smoothly. There is never any harm in asking, "Given what we want to accomplish, how many different ways of accomplishing it can we find?" Brainstorming strategies is one of the best ways of assuring good choices.

• **Make sure that strategies are clear and specific.** Strategies, like goals, need to be clear and specific if they are to move organizational players to action.

> EXAMPLE: The manager of an accounting unit in UIA conducted a meeting to share the results of an attitude survey with her staff. She said, "The attitude survey shows that people are dissatisfied because they are allowed such little initiative. I'd actually like to see more initiative here. So please feel free to be creative about the things we do here. The important thing is to accomplish our work programs and achieve our objectives. The way we go about it is not that important, at least within limits."

This is not as much of a caricature as it may at first seem. First, the preferred scenario—increased initiative at the service of greater productivity and improved quality of work life—needs to be clarified. Questions like "What would increased initiative look like in this accounting unit?" Second, brainstorming should produce a range of clear ways of moving toward increased initiative. One possible strategy would be for members of the unit to identify and interview clients (e.g., people in the airline responsible for establishing and administering departmental unit budgets). An analysis of their needs would lead to new products (such as software products) and services (such as workshops on the use of spreadsheets in drawing up and reformulating budgets). At monthly meetings, possible new products and services would be reviewed and the best adopted. This strategy is much more specific than a casual injunction to be more creative.

- **Link the strategy to the preferred outcome.** The relationship between strategies and preferred outcomes must be capable of being verified. If the impact of a course of action is not capable of being verified, then it is not a viable strategy. Some organizational players, beguiled by the newness or creative nature of strategies themselves, pursue them without linking them to the outcomes of the preferred scenario. The director of welfare programs for an East Coast state once remarked to me, "That's just what we do. We try every new program that comes down the Federal pike. It usually doesn't work, is abandoned, and then we try the next one. We have no clear public-welfare policy, just a lot of programs floating around." In this case, there was nothing to which the strategies could be linked.

- **Choose realistic strategies.** The course of action must be within the resources of the client, under his or her control, environmentally possible, and owned by the client. What happened in Poland is a depressing example of the lack of realistic means to produce a preferred scenario. Poland was basically an agricultural economy when the planners decided that it should specialize in heavy industry. However, Poland had no industrial tradition and it lacked the requisite reservoir of worker and management skills. Cook (1987) states:

> In launching these [industrial] projects, nobody worried much about how dependent the country was becoming on imported components, subassemblies, spare parts and raw materials, an oversight that would cost Poland dearly when the money finally ran out. (p. 75)

Factories were shut down because no one had the $300 for a needed part, and the foreign desk of the Polish National Bank was shut down for a week because there was no printer paper. In sum, the preferred industrialization scenario called for strategies that were not realistic. There is, of course, a difference between realism and selling a client short. Strategies that make clients "stretch" for a valued goal can be very useful.

EXAMPLE: The CEO of the smaller computer firm mentioned earlier (which was in jeopardy because of a downturn in the computer business) soon realized that one of his survival strategies, asking people from a number of different departments to go out and sell the company's products, involved work for which they had not been prepared. Many of those asked balked at the task. His revised strategy focused on volunteers who spent time at industry shows where the company had a booth. Before going, the volunteers learned about the products and while there, worked with representatives who showed them the ropes. This prepared them much better for the sales role. Many of them volunteered to sell after this experience.

Sometimes education and training are necessary to make a strategy realistic.

• **Choose strategies that contribute substantially to outcomes.** Sometimes goals do not get accomplished because strategies, while realistic, are not substantial enough to move the preferred agenda along in any significant way. The result is that people, after trying weak strategies, give up and say that the agenda itself is not feasible.

EXAMPLE: A directive was sent to all managers asking them to do whatever they could to take advantage of extremely low air fares because of an ongoing fare war. Since getting the lower fares meant staying over one Saturday, most managers dismissed the memo as meaningless: "I go out on Wednesdays and come back on Fridays." However, frequent travelers could have taken advantage of the low fares by buying two overlapping sets of tickets at a time—one set originating in the city where the company was based, another originating in the destination city. For instance, one set might be for a Chicago-to-Denver roundtrip starting out on Wednesday, June 1, and returning to Chicago on Friday, June 10. The other set would be for a Denver-to-Chicago roundtrip starting Friday, June 3, and returning to Denver on Wednesday, June 8.

The preferred outcome, was, of course, reduced travel costs. The means used—an exhortation to travelers to use the lower fares—proved ineffective. If the memo had included a couple of examples of how easily money could be saved and an offer to help in arranging the lowest fares, it might have made a difference.

• **Make sure that the players own the strategies.** Strategies, like preferred-scenario outcomes, must be owned by those responsible for carrying them out.

EXAMPLE: A mid-sized company was attempting to restructure itself in order to deliver its services to its customers more effectively. A group of organization consultants were hired to help with the task. Three task forces were established to determine the ways in which three different areas of the institution needed to be restructured. A pattern developed. The consultants would arrive at the same time the task forces began their meetings. However, the consultants would closet themselves and then emerge every once in a while to tell one or another of the task forces what they should do. The members of the task forces were obedient for a while, but eventually they rebelled and told the consultants they were not interested in their advice.

The consultants failed to realize that they were working with intelligent men and women who resented being patronized. If organizational players participate in the generation and choice of strategies, they are much more likely to own them. Perhaps some excellent ideas generated by the consultants went to waste because of the way they went about the consultation process.

• **Keep strategies in line with organizational values and with the values of those charged with implementing them.** If strategies run counter to business, organizational, or personal values, the likelihood of their being avoided or sabotaged is high.

EXAMPLE: A small appliance firm was not weathering the downturn in its industry very well. One of the reasons it was in trouble was that risk taking in this firm was countercultural. One of the means chosen to weather the storm was sending people from a variety of departments out on the streets as sales people (similar to the strategy adopted by the computer company mentioned earlier.) Since personal security and aversion to risk taking were values in place, the newly ordained sales representatives did not take well to what they felt was an even riskier business.

It is not just a question of overt or espoused values. Strategies that violate the covert values of the organization or individuals within it are at risk.

• **Set strategies in a reasonable time frame.** This is the purpose of formulating an explicit action plan. Action planning will be considered in Chapter 15.

EXPLORING THE CONSEQUENCES OF STRATEGIES

Some strategies, while possible, fail as best-fit strategies because of their consequences, especially longer-term consequences. Screaming at my boss may help me manage my pent-up frustration in the short term, but the longer-term consequences should give me pause. Failing to assess longer-term consequences is a common blind spot in change strategies.

EXAMPLE: Another area of concern is UIA's relationship with the unions, especially the unions of a relatively high-cost carrier recently acquired by UIA. The new CEO brought with him a union-buster reputation. He negotiated a number of give-backs with the unions of another airline in which he held an executive position. The consequences of going jaw to jaw with the unions would probably be strikes and a climate of turmoil that would affect both employees and passengers. UIA had enough cash to outlast a strike and in the long run could even fold the newly acquired airline and merely take over its planes and routes. However, all of this would project an image of ruthlessness that the CEO and board saw as inadvisable for both social and business reasons. Therefore, the unions were invited to join deliberations on assimilating the newly acquired airline and fitting it into the vision of a low-cost, low-fare, profitable airline that was positioning itself for the long haul.

Best-fit strategies are not the same as perfect-fit strategies. It often happens that there are both positive and negative consequences for any set of strategies. If this is the case, then the trade-offs involved need to be scrutinized in terms of risk and the probability of success.

Risk and the Probability of Success: Four Approaches

In choosing strategies, change agents need to evaluate the risk involved and determine whether the risk is proportional to the probability of success. Gelatt, Varenhorst, and Carey (1972) suggest four approaches to dealing with risk and the probability of success: the wish approach, the safe approach, the escape approach, and the combination approach.

1. The Wish Approach. In the "wish" strategy the organizational players choose a course of action that they hope will lead to the accomplishment of preferred-scenario outcomes, but the choice is made regardless of risk, cost, or probability of success. This strategy is used sometimes by organizations in panic.

> EXAMPLE: One of the airlines bought out by UIA had itself bought an airline without, it would seem, reckoning the consequences. This low-cost, no-frills airline wanted to become a successful coast-to-coast operator. It did so overnight by purchasing another low-cost, low-fare operator in the western part of the United States. Some analysts say they paid too much for the airline, failed to determine that they were mutually incompatible, grew too quickly by the purchase to maintain control over the vastly increased network, and pushed the purchase through without first bringing some of its own growing-pain problems under control. In sum, the airline was in a panic to grow and chose a strategy that was too risky, too costly, and too lacking in probability of success.

In the wish approach, the organization operates blindly, using strategies without taking into account their feasibility. Organizations that work hard at change and still get nowhere might well be using wish strategies; that is, they may be persevering in using strategies they prefer but which are of doubtful efficacy.

2. The Safe Approach. In the "safe" approach, the organization chooses only safe courses of action with a high degree of probability of producing at least limited success.

> EXAMPLE: While other department stores—in order to retain or even increase their market share—were moving quickly into specialty retailing, one mid-sized chain known for its solid, no-nonsense goods, merely redecorated its stores and freshened up its advertising and catalog. More radical moves were seen as countercultural. Its "new look" fooled no one and customers continued to flock to the department chains that had introduced a whole range of specialty stores within their larger stores. The chain in question continued to lose market share.

The trouble with the "safe" approach is that it places limitations on the kinds of preferred scenarios that can be pursued. Outcomes have to be tailored to safe and probable means. Organizations may well end up being safe but also sorry.

3. The Escape Approach. In the the escape approach, organizations choose means that are likely to help them avoid the worst possible result; it minimizes the maximum danger.

> EXAMPLE: One year, when the economy was in recession, the owner of an independent supermarket was faced with severe cash-flow problems. His plight was exacerbated by the opening of a store by a large chain in his area of the city. He opted for a whole range of cost-cutting strategies. He laid off a number of workers, cut back on store hours, and reduced his inventory to the barest minimum. For him, being declared in default by any of his creditors was the worst possible scenario. His strategies backfired. The poorly stocked shelves gave his store a hollow feeling. Business dropped off dramatically. Before long he was forced into bankruptcy.

The obvious problem with such an approach is that it is based on avoidance. The preferred scenario is the avoidance of some kind of calamity, and not a vision of something better. As we see in the case above, adopting escape tactics can sometimes even precipitate the catastrophe that organizational actors are trying to avoid. The escape approach prevents new learning from taking place.

4. The Combination Approach. In the combination approach, organizations choose courses of action which, although they involve risk, both minimize danger and increase the probability of accomplishing an agenda in the way and to the degree they desire.

> EXAMPLE: During a downturn in the automotive industry, one of the largest players used it as an opportunity to restructure itself, eliminate layers of middle managers, and cut costs in a whole host of ways. At the same time, it designed and delivered a range of new products that took the competition by surprise. It emerged from the recession leaner and competitively meaner.

This combination approach is the most difficult to apply, for it involves the ability and heart needed to clarify preferred-scenario outcomes, to review and reaffirm organizational and individual values, to rank a variety of action strategies according to these values, and to predict the probable results of a given package of strategies. Sometimes organizations have neither the time nor the will for this kind of detailed work. The strategies listed in Step III-A (in Chapter 13) for the United International Airways' performance planning and appraisal project all fall in the best-fit category. The following example illustrates some poor choices.

> EXAMPLE: Following are some of the strategies that UAI considered but which did *not* meet the criteria listed in Step III-B. The reasons they would have been *poor* choices are also given.
>
> • *Make the personnel department the PPA project management unit.* This is a poor strategy because PPA will not work unless *line managers* own it and promote it.
>
> • *Give each manager a detailed PPA blueprint that he or she is to follow step by step.* This is eliminated because it robs line managers of their autonomy.
>
> • *Just give the broadest of guidelines to managers and let each manager or each unit do its own version of PPA.* This fails the test because line managers need some kind of framework they can tailor. Merely giving extremely broad guidelines is the same as giving an order to "go and do it."
>
> • *Start the PPA process with lower-level managers and supervisors.* This strategy sends the wrong message—that PPA is for "you folks down there." The PPA system is fragile. Explicit modeling at the top is needed. The people at the top need to be the first PPA project directors.
>
> • *Put the appraisal system in order first without worrying about the two other parts of PPA—performance planning and ongoing feedback. After all, that's where many managers, supervisors, and staff have great difficulty.* This is rejected because appraisal is meaningless without the clear objectives agreed

to in the performance-planning process. And if there is no ongoing feedback, the burden on the appraisal meeting is too much.

• *Have the personnel department monitor the implementation of the system in order to ensure accountability.* This promotes the image of Personnel as ogre. But more basically, line managers and supervisors—together with those they are managing and supervising—are accountable. Make Personnel the monitor only if you want to destroy commitment to the PPA system.

• *Have a performance plan for each unit but do not have those who work in the unit do individual performance plans. This will make things simpler.* This is a bad idea because it stops the PPA process half way. It sends the wrong signal to workers—PPA is nothing more than a control device invented and imposed by management.

• *Have managers assign objectives to individuals based on the unit performance plan.* This robs workers of participation in the decisions affecting their lives and sabotages accountability.

In short, strategies such as these were deemed as unrealistic or inadequate and therefore eliminated from the pool of strategies from which the implementation plan for the PPA process was to be drawn.

ACTION AS STRATEGY SAMPLING

Throughout a change process, organizational actors can determine the feasibility of the kinds of strategies that are to comprise the ultimate plan (Step III-C) by trying them out. This is called strategy sampling and is part of the action orientation of Model A.

EXAMPLE: The founders of a mental health clinic, which was set up in what some called an "impossible" part of a midwestern city, decided to try a whole range of programs in their first year before establishing the mission and major categories of services of the agency. They simply did not know what combination of programs would suit the needs of the area. After a year in which they allowed themselves some relatively risky experiments, they formulated a mission that targeted high-risk groups and individuals for special treatment.

Some organizations, of course, might use strategy sampling as a way of putting off action. Nevertheless, if strategies are costly in terms of time, energy, and/or money, sampling to see how effective they might be and how they fit resources, values, and preferences could make sense.

15

Step III-C:
Formulating Plans

29. current step in MIS Strategy

Some strategies are quite simple and there is no need to work out a step-by-step procedure to accomplish some preferred-scenario outcomes. Other strategies are more complicated, and organizational players need to determine what steps need to be taken and in what order. Working out a step-by-step plan or action program increases the probability that the change effort will move forward. Figure 15-1 adds the final step to Model B, organizing best-fit strategies into a coherent plan.

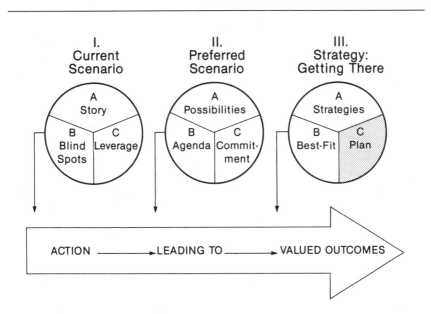

Figure 15-1. A Model for Organization Change

Below are a number of reasons why action plans help attain preferred-scenario goals.

• **Evaluating Realism.** Action plans provide a framework for evaluating the realism and adequacy of new scenarios and goals. For instance, only when the administrators of a hospital began to formulate explicit plans for a new wing did they realize that it would divert their attention from reformulating the mission of the institution and the pressing problem of filling beds. A new wing, though long envisioned, was the last thing needed right then. The turmoil in the health care industries suggested other priorities. Turning strategies into plans helps further evaluate the realism of the strategies themselves.

• **Finding Better Strategies.** Formulating action plans helps organizations search for more useful ways of accomplishing goals, that is, even better strategies. An airline experiencing unrest among baggage handlers and ticket sellers at a time of an upsurge in its business had decided to try to manage the problem by running human relations training groups for workers at one of its most troubled airports. As the manager and his staff worked out plans for the training program with a consultant, it dawned on everyone that the issue was not the operators but the supervisors. They did not know how to supervise now that the entire system had gone taut. They quickly brainstormed ways of helping supervisors cope better.

• **Setting Realistic Time Frames.** Plans help organizational actors determine how much time will be required to accomplish objectives. A consulting firm was asked to do a culture audit of a mid-sized hotel chain about to embark on an organization restructuring program. The restructuring was long overdue and therefore was to be done as quickly as possible. When the consultants sat down with their plans for the audit, it became clear that what they proposed would take much longer than the restructuring project. They had to settle for a much less ambitious audit.

• **Estimating Psychological Costs.** Plans help change agents determine the psychological costs involved in moving toward a preferred-scenario goal. When the person to whom the task of closing a plant for a large manufacturer had been delegated organized his strategies into a plan, he quickly realized that the psychological costs for both those working on the closing and the community in which it was located would be enormous. He presented his case to headquarters and was given a longer time frame for the closing.

• **Determining Needed Resources.** Plans help organizations determine what kind of resources, especially human resources, they will need to accomplish goals. Members of a voting watch-dog group wanted to supplement the work of regular polling-place judges in an important election with "sentinels" of their own. In spelling out plans for the training and placement of these supplemental forces, they realized they did not have the resources for the training needed—they would run out of time, money, and personnel. In a quick shift they worked out an agreement with the city to have their people receive the same training that the regular judges received. They then merely supplemented this training, pointing out specific polling-place problems affecting specific areas of the city and ways of coping with them.

• **Discovering Snags.** Formulating clear plans helps change agents uncover unanticipated snags or obstacles to the accomplishment of goals. Only in working out the details of a crash training program for flight attendants did staff members of United International Airways realize that certain union rules would prevent them from shortening the program as planned. They immediately met with union officials and worked out an agreement by which those trained in the "short" course would return for further training within six months. This met UIA's need for attendants for the summer rush and the union's need for a complete training program.

• **Identifying the Need for Outside Help.** Plans identify areas in which organizational players might need help from consultants or other professionals. In formulating plans for a fund-raising program, the members of a church soon realized that people with computer expertise would help enormously. They quickly sought out church members with the required skills in handling data bases.

As suggested earlier, plans help change agents make time an ally instead of an enemy. They help answer questions such as: What needs to be done today? What needs to be done tomorrow? How can these steps be best organized to get us where we want to go?

SHAPING THE PLAN:
DEVELOPING SUBGOALS AND STRATEGIES

If a problem situation or change project is complex, any given preferred-scenario goal may have a number of subgoals. A subgoal is a step toward a larger goal. In larger projects, the coordination and integration of all steps at the service of the preferred scenario is a demanding task.

Other things being equal, the simpler the plan the better, provided it helps the organization achieve its goals. However, simplicity is not an end in itself. The question is not whether or not any given plan is complicated or whether it is well shaped or organized. If complicated plans are broken down into subgoals and their accompanying strategies, they are as capable of being achieved, if the time frame is realistic, as simpler ones.

Consider the outplacement counseling program that constitutes part of the overall plant-closing plan of a large manufacturer. The work of the counselors is not to find jobs for those working at the plant, but to help them find jobs. This means helping them coordinate their efforts in a plan. In schematic form action-program shaping looks like this:

Subprogram #1 leads to subgoal #1.
Subprogram #2 leads to subgoal #2.
Subprogram #n (the last in the sequence) leads to the accomplishment of the major goal.

This can be applied to the overall plan the job hunter needs to follow. Note that the steps are outlined in terms of a succession of *outcomes* instead of a succession of actions. Goals must be set first, then actions follow.

Subgoal #1: Kind of job wanted determined.
Subgoal #2: Resume written.
Subgoal #3: Job possibilities canvassed.
Subgoal #4: Best job prospects identified.
Subgoal #5: Job interviews arranged.
Subgoal #6: Job interviews completed.
Subgoal #7: Job offers assessed.
Subgoal #8: Job chosen.
Preferred outcome: New job started.

A plan should have the detail needed to achieve the objective—in this case, satisfactory employment.

Since each of these major steps represents outcomes or accomplishments that are preparatory for the next step, actions leading to these outcomes could also be identified. That is, for each subgoal a step-by-step program or subplan needs to be established. For instance, the program for the subgoal "job possibilities canvassed" might include such things as reading the help-wanted section of the local papers, contacting friends or acquaintances who might be able to offer jobs or provide leads, asking friends to read the bulletin boards at local factories, visiting employment agencies, and other job-canvassing strategies (see the list of over fifty strategies listed in the discussion of brainstorming in Chapter 13).

A subgoal or accomplishment must fulfill the same requirements as a goal, that is, it must be:

• **Stated as a clear, specific, behavioral accomplishment.** "Job possibilities thoroughly canvassed" is an outcome that is stated as a clear accomplishment.

• **Adequate, that is, clearly related both to the next subgoal and to the major outcome toward which it is directed.** If a person looking for a new job does a good job at canvassing job possibilities, then she or he is ready to pick out the best prospects (the next subgoal in the program) and is moving toward the major goal of getting a job.

• **Within the control of the person responsible for the outcome.** The outplacement program leaves it up to the person looking for a new job to take responsibility for canvassing job possibilities. Most people, with a little coaching, can engage in a number of job-canvassing strategies on their own.

• **Realistic, that is, within the resources and capabilities of the person responsible for the outcome and in keeping with the environmental constraints within which the person is operating.** The person looking for a new job might need some encouragement from the outplacement counselor, but it is assumed that he or she has the resources needed to search out job possibilities.

• **Compatible with the other subgoals of the program and with relevant values.** Job possibilities must first be discovered before job seekers can decide which ones look most promising. For some, moving away from the area is not feasible because of family values. Therefore, an intensive search for local jobs needs to be mounted.

• **Capable of being verified.** Job seekers need to know when they have fulfilled the requirements of an adequate job canvass.

• **Assigned a reasonable time frame for completion.** Job canvassing could go on forever. Time limits need to be set.

It is clear that it is not necessary to apply each of these criteria explicitly to each subgoal. Planning is not an end in itself; it is a means to help actors move toward preferred-scenario outcomes.

CONTINGENCY PLANS

Life being what it is, the chosen plan or some part of it might not work as well as expected. Therefore, it is wise to formulate back-up or contingency plans. We have already seen the need for contingency scenarios in Stage II. Contingency plans are needed especially when organizations choose a high-risk strategy to achieve a critical goal.

EXAMPLE: The embattled mayor of large city in the West of the United States geared his re-election campaign to detailing what he saw as the flaws in the administration of his principal opponent, who then became ill and dropped out of the race. The opponent, who was considered a second-class candidate, had been campaigning on the "issues": unemployment, an eroding industrial base, patronage, and a range of quality-of-life concerns. The mayor was caught short. His TV commercials and campaign literature centered around the defects of his major opponent. All of a sudden, the second-class candidate appeared attractive to many voters. There were no contingency plans for a different kind of campaign. The mayor and his forces had to improvise, and they improvised poorly.

Merely having back-up plans helps prop up the entire change project. If the grand plan goes awry, organizational players might begin to lose heart. However, if everyone knows that contingency plans are ready, momentum need not be lost.

SOME PROBLEMS ASSOCIATED WITH DEVELOPING PLANS

There are a number of problems associated with the development of plans to reach subgoals and goals. Two are reviewed briefly here: resisting the work of developing plans and getting lost in details.

Resistance to Planning

Some organizations set exciting objectives but then resist the work of setting up effective step-by-step programs because it either seems too complicated or they feel that they can "wing it." Some organizational players who work more intuitively see detailed planning as overly rational. The point is that some systematic framework should guide action.

EXAMPLE: UIA's cabin-crew training staff was exposed to an exciting new training program currently being used by a foreign carrier. It had a strong socialization or enculturation component. It was clear that it could be adapted to UIA's needs quite easily. The trainers looked at some videotapes and paged through some written materials. Most of them thought that they could "borrow a lot of good stuff" from the program. They immediately implemented some of the ideas, each in his or her own way. The trainees become confused, especially when they found out from people in other training groups that they were learning something different.

What was needed here was a reworking of the training program so that the new ideas could be integrated. Although intuition can be a valuable resource, acting on intuition, especially in the case of complicated problem situations, is courting disaster. Put more positively, intuition that is guided by the logic of planning is likely to be more useful than raw intuition.

Getting Lost in Details

A common mistake made by novices who use planning and program-development technology is to become too detailed.

> EXAMPLE: A UIA manager was glad he was given the opportunity to tailor the generic performance planning and appraisal framework to his own unit. He designed what it was going to look like in his unit together with a step-by-step installation plan. However, the PPA process he designed was overloaded with detail as was the installation plan. Furthermore, he moved too quickly. His staff, who had not been asked to participate in the design, rebelled. Many of them blamed the PPA system itself and resisted even simpler forms.

It is relatively easy to learn how to break problems and goals into smaller parts and to chain together the steps needed to accomplish both subgoals and major goals. This keeps people from becoming disheartened because they are lost in details. Acquiring and using planning and program-development skills is like learning any other kind of skill. At first it feels awkward, but with practice the entire process becomes much easier.

THE PERFORMANCE PLANNING AND APPRAISAL PROJECT AT UIA

Once the strategies for the implementation of the PPA project at UIA had been chosen, they needed to be organized into an implementation plan.

EXAMPLE: Because of the scope of the PPA change effort, the action plan at UIA proved to be long and detailed. Some of the highlights of plan were as follows:

- **Communication.** A number of strategies were used for the CEO and the PPA task force to keep everyone at UIA informed. A PPA hotline was established to answer questions from managers. Each manager became responsible for keeping his or her staff abreast of PPA developments. General guidelines for drawing up performance plans were issued. A format for both unit and individual planning was shared, but it was a flexible format that could be adapted by each unit to its needs.

- **Training.** A complete training program in performance planning was established. The CEO and his vice presidents received this training first and immediately set about the task of completing the performance plans for their organizational units and their individual plans. As they were doing their plans, those reporting to the vice presidents were trained.

- **Cascading.** A cascading strategy of training and performance planning was adopted. Once a manager was trained, he or she was responsible for seeing to it that those who reported to him or her were trained and that they followed up with performance plans.

- **Feedback.** When individual managers completed their unit and individual plans, they received training in establishing a culture of feedback in their units and in giving and receiving feedback. Managers became responsible for two-way feedback. They were expected to receive it from their subordinates; they were expected to give it to their bosses. This training, too, cascaded through the system. It included training in the communication skills needed to provide both confirmatory and corrective feedback. Self-feedback was central to this training and was related to clarity of performance goals and outcome indicators.

- **Appraisals.** Finally, training in conducting appraisals of both projects and individuals was cascaded through the system. Appraisals were presented as opportunities for summaries, integration, and fine tuning. They were seen as the beginning of the next round of performance-planning dialogs.

These were the major steps in the plan. Obviously the implementation plans for communication, training, the writing of performance plans, feedback sessions, and appraisal conferences were much more detailed.

ACTION IN STEP III-C

↑ means to getting to outcomes

~~Action plans are not the same as outcome-producing action.~~ If plans are poorly conceived and overloaded with detail, they can squash initiative. On the other hand, if plans are good, they act ~~as triggers and create channels for action.~~ In reality in the best change projects, mini-plans are being drawn up and executed right from the beginning. Finally, when it is time to formalize an implementation plan, change agents can draw on the experience of those who have already acted, learning from both their successes and their failures.

16

Action II:
The Transition—
Implementing Plans

In effective change programs, outcome-producing action—as we have emphasized over and over—starts from the very beginning of the project and continues throughout. These "little" actions lead the organization "generally west" during the diagnosis and planning process; they constitute one of the best signs of the organization's commitment to change. However, once a formal plan has been drawn up, the formal transition phase begins, that is, the transition from the current to the preferred scenario. The formal transition phase is a critical time, because people must get the ordinary work of the system done and at the same time implement the changes that constitute the preferred scenario. Therefore, this last chapter focuses on the transition phase, on what needs to be done to move from planning to implementation. Figure 16-1 designates the large "action" arrow in the graphic presentation of Model B as the transition phase (see Beckhard, 1985 and Beckhard & Harris, 1987).

Just as the model itself can be used to manage resistance to proposing and planning change, so now it can be used to solve or manage the problems that accompany implementation.

EXAMPLE: At one university the members of several programs (the organizational studies program, a group in the communications department interested in organizational change, a group from the school of education interested in organizations, two members of the urban studies department, and two sociologists whose specialty was applied sociology) got together to establish an organizational consultancy and training institute that would reach out to clients outside the univer-

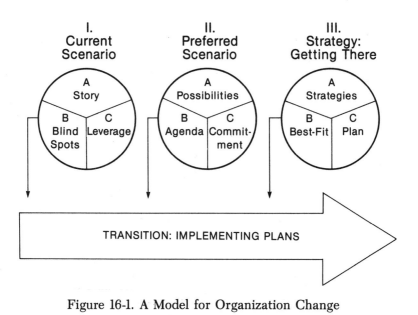

Figure 16-1. A Model for Organization Change

sity. The institute would not only sell its services to a variety or organizations, including churches, schools, and human-services agencies, but it would also provide a center for internships and research for the students involved in these programs. The group presented its proposal to the administration of the university and, after several meetings, were told that the university was, "in principle," committed to the idea but needed some questions answered. The group answered the questions, but the administration kept throwing up one bureaucratic hurdle after another.

At this point the groups became frustrated and decided to use the change model to manage their frustrations. Their preferred scenario was a firm decision from the university of "go" or "no go." Merely coping with one bureaucratic obstacle after another, while giving the illusion that the project was moving forward, was a waste of time. The strategy they chose was a confrontation meeting with the president of the university. At this meeting the president pointed out the conservative nature of the university, admitted that some of his aides were worried about the possibility of malpractice suits and the cost of insurance, and hinted that some influential people (probably from the business school) were opposed to the idea in principle. All this added up to a no-go decision, even though he seemed to want to leave the door open. While this was not the preferred decision for the interested groups, it did satisfy their need for closure. They stopped all efforts at handling the bureaucratic hurdles and channeled their efforts in different directions.

In this case, plans were all in place, but implementation was stymied at every turn. A simple application of the model itself enabled them to move on quickly to more fruitful pursuits. As seen in *Change-Agent Skills A: Assessing and Designing Excellence* (Egan, 1988), effective leaders not only turn visions into realistic agendas and arouse enthusiasm for these agendas by the very way in which they communicate them to others, but they also create a ferment of problem solving and learning around these agendas and make sure that organizational actors *persist* until the agendas are accomplished. In many ways the transition phase is about *tactics* and *logistics*. Tactics is the art of being able to adapt a plan to the immediate situation; it is the art of persistence. This includes being able to change the plan on the spot in order to handle unforeseen complications. *Logistics* is the art of being able to provide the resources needed for the implementation of any given plan when they are required. These have already been at work in the informal actions that have cropped up during the formal diagnosis and planning phases. The organizational literature is filled with examples of organizational "intrapreneurs" (Pinchot, 1985) who have begged, borrowed, and stolen resources (logistics) to move projects ahead informally despite a whole host of organizational constraints (tactics).

INERTIA AND ENTROPY

The two principal enemies during the transition phase are our old nemeses, inertia and entropy. Inertia has already been mentioned— the inertia that undercuts both planning for change and the kinds of informal actions that need to permeate the entire change process. However, having a master plan, even a very realistic master plan, does not automatically eliminate inertia.

EXAMPLE: I was asked to sit with the administrator of a thirteen-hospital health-care system and the members of the board to discuss possible changes in the policies and procedures of the system. It was soon evident that the administrator ran the show with a rather heavy hand. During our discussion of some of their concerns—though the administrator intimated that this meeting had not been *her* idea—I began to get one of those feelings that plague consultants: "Somebody has been here before me." And so I eventually asked: "Have you engaged in exercises similar to this before?" The administrator opened one of the drawers of her desk, pulled out a rather forbiddingly thick tome, set it on the desk in front of me, and said, "Oh, certainly. There was a group of consultants here just over a year ago. Here is the final report. I must admit, however, that we've been extremely busy and haven't had a chance to do much about its recommendations." So much for organizational readiness for change and the "power" of a formal change plan.

Perhaps the main reason plans do not work is that they are never tried. Obviously the administrator had been opposed to the project from the very beginning. Dragging her feet was enough to prevent any serious push for the implementation of the recommendations. Poorly conceived change projects deserve both inertia and entropy, but even good ones are stalked by both.

In order to understand the major problems of the transition phase, most of us need only to reflect on our own experience in trying to implement programs. We make plans and they seem realistic to us. We start into the initial steps of a program with a good deal of enthusiasm. However, we soon run into tedium, obstacles, and complications. What seemed so easy in the planning stage now seems quite difficult. We become discouraged, flounder, recover our balance, flounder again, and finally give up, offering ourselves rationalizations as to why we did not want to accomplish those goals anyway. Inertia and entropy do not necessarily signal ill will. Rather they are part of the human condition. If we don't get them, they will get us. As Ferguson (1980) notes, both individuals and social systems often feel at risk during the transition state. It is the "trapeze" feeling. During the action or transition phase, organizations need to let go one trapeze bar, that is, familiar but unproductive patterns of behavior, and grab hold of a new trapeze bar, new and more productive patterns of behavior. Weick (1979) talks about an innovation's "threshold of vulnerability," the critical time when it can be resented or go unnoticed and thus fail. Kirkpatrick (1985) notes that new norms are always weaker than those they replace. This results in a tendency to backslide toward the norm that previously prevailed (see Blake & Mouton, 1982).

FORCE-FIELD ANALYSIS:
FOREWARNED IS FOREARMED

Force-field analysis (Lewin, 1969; Spier, 1973), despite its somewhat sophisticated name, is conceptually simple. It can be a useful tool in helping discover and cope with transition-related obstacles, on the one hand, and develop transition-related resources, on the other. The analysis focuses on two basic questions:

TACTICS • Now that we have our plan, what can possibly get in our way?

LOGISTICS • Now that we have our plan, what further resources might we harness?

This process is illustrated in Figure 16-2. Gottfredson (1984) suggests several reasons why such an analysis is useful: First, it helps change agents challenge environmental blind spots: "What are we overlooking? Let's step back and take a harder look at what can help us or hinder us during the transition phase." Brainstorming is useful here. Second, force-field analysis helps us assess forces that are not in our direct control with a view to taking advantage of them. For instance, Chrysler's striking turnaround capitalized on an upswing in the economy. Third, the analysis can surface further strategies for implementing the plan.

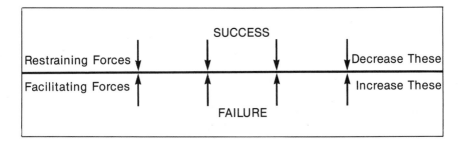

Figure 16-2. Force-Field Analysis

Restraining Forces. Restraining forces are the obstacles that might be encountered during the transition. The identification of possible obstacles to the implementation of a program helps to forewarn organizational actors.

> EXAMPLE: One of the principal restraining forces in the implementation of UIA's performance planning and appraisal system was the residual cynicism concerning the system's predecessor, the annual evaluation review (AER). The AER had become a joke. In fact, PPA was to be an attempt at modernizing and resetting this system. The AER focused, as the name implies, on the end-of-the-year review and said little, if anything, about performance planning and ongoing feedback. The PPA task force brainstormed a host of other possible obstacles.

If organizational actors are aware of some of the wrinkles that can accompany any given plan of action, they will be less disoriented when they encounter them. This part of the force-field analysis process is, at its best, a straightforward census of probable pitfalls rather than a self-defeating search for every possible thing that could go wrong.

Once a restraining force is identified, ways of coping with it can be explored. Sometimes simply being aware of a pitfall is enough to help people mobilize their resources to handle it. At other times a more explicit coping strategy is needed.

> EXAMPLE: The strategy used to counteract the cynicism around the AER at UIA was, principally, admitting it formally. One of the PPA planning communications discussed the AER frankly, noted its limitations, talked about how it had been used to try to move incompetent people from one department to another, and outlined other forms of cynicism that surrounded it.

Restraining forces can come from the structure, processes, and procedures of organizations themselves, from individual organizational actors, and from a wide range of environmental factors.

Facilitating Forces. In a more positive vein, force-field analysis can help change agents identify important trends and resources to be used in implementing programs. Stein (1980) suggests that action programs need to be butressed by "rachets," that is, strategies and tactics designed to keep programs in place, to keep them from falling apart. Brainstorming facilitating forces can help identify the rachets needed during the transition phase. Facilitating forces can be persons, places, things, trends, and the like.

EXAMPLE: Paradoxically, one of the principal facilitating forces for the UIA PPA program was the confusion caused by the airline's sudden growth, mainly through acquisitions, and its need to restructure. People were in need of some kind of framework to make sense of the confusion and provide direction. PPA did provide one useful framework.

Once a facilitating force is identified, ways of taking advantage of it can be explored.

EXAMPLE: The PPA task force sold the new system to managers and supervisors as a way of handling the confusion surrounding the acquisitions and restructuring. They provided examples of how PPA was already being used by many managers in a variety of departments to pull together their teams.

Force-field analysis is a way of applying Step I-C, challenging blind spots and developing new perspectives, in a most pragmatic way, to the implementation phase of the change process.

Systematic Steps in the Use of Force-Field Analysis. The following steps may be used in bringing force-field analysis to bear on the transition stage.

- List all the restraining forces that might stand in the way of implementing a plan.
- List all the facilitating forces at work.
- Underline the forces in each list (facilitating and restraining) that seem most critical with respect to carrying out the action plan. This helps simplify the process. Some are more important than others.
- Identify strategies for reducing significant restraining forces and for strengthening and utilizing significant facilitating forces.

TRANSITION PRINCIPLES

The following principles—both do's and don'ts—will help in moving from the current to the preferred scenario.

Get an effective transition manager or team. Beckhard and Harris (1987) stress the importance of getting the right person or persons to oversee the transition. This person may or may not be the top person in the organization. Managing the transition is best placed in competent, sensitive, persistent, and responsive hands. The appointment of a transition manager or team sends an important signal to the rest of the organization: "This person [this team] embodies how we feel about this change project."

> EXAMPLE: One mid-sized organization, involved in its first major restructuring in fifteen years, created a temporary vice presidency to manage the change. The person chosen for this position was from operations, was not already a vice president, and was highly respected in the organization. His mandate was one of coordination and facilitation, not of monitoring and control. The team he chose was a diagonal slice of the organization. Team members retained their other jobs. Establishing such a "parallel structure" (Stein & Kanter, 1980) sent clear messages to the entire organization, such as "We're very serious about this renewal" and "This is a total team effort."

Very often the most important job of the transition manager or team is to guard the perimeter. That is, while the rest of the people get on with the process of change, the transition manager keeps the world from interfering. Ideally this guard-the-perimeter role should cascade throughout the managerial structure of the organization.

Make sure that the resources needed to effect the transition are available. When planners draw up their formal plan for moving to the preferred scenario, they also indicate the resources needed to implement the plan. This can be called "Resourcing I." However, since *tactics* is the art of adapting a plan to the inevitable twists and turns that any plan will encounter, there needs to be a kind of tactical resourcing, which can be called "Resourcing II." It is deadly to ask people to do a job and then withhold the resources they need to do it; yet this happens quite frequently in change projects, especially when the resources needed were not foreseen in the original plan.

EXAMPLE: Rather severe cost-cutting measures were announced to the workers in an insurance company. Budgets were to be cut, positions eliminated, and those remaining were asked to become more productive. The members of one department devised small-team approaches to process new insurance policies. Their efforts demonstrated that the small-team approach was both faster and more efficient. To work at maximum efficiency, however, they needed a micro-computer with a number of terminals or several linked personal computers. They demonstrated the cost effectiveness of their requests quite clearly. However, one of the cost-cutting measures was a hold on the purchase of any new office equipment. Even when the department demonstrated that the new computers would pay for themselves within four months, the policy was not modified.

There is a need to take a comprehensive, longer-term view of the change project. Under-resourcing change efforts can quickly lead to a loss in morale. Sometimes training or retraining is an important resource, especially when people are being asked to do jobs they did not do before. One of the major complaints at United International Airways was that veteran flight attendants were being asked to train new flight attendants without themselves receiving any training in instructional methodology.

Establish a climate of problem solving and learning around the agenda. As we have seen, this is what leaders do. They continually encourage implementers to see the agenda as a challenge, to tinker with it until it works, to use it as a stimulus for learning.

EXAMPLE: An Internal Revenue Service manager suggested that there was to be an open competition in the IRS on inventive ways of tapping into and taxing the "underground economy." Since the ways of operating in that economy are countless, he saw the competition as ongoing. In his own office he tried a mini-version of the competition. Part of the staff played the role of underground "economists," while others played their normal IRS role. The former were amazed by the many ways they discovered for playing the underground economists. The activity helped the staff understand the mentality of the underground player more thoroughly, and it produced a range of strategies for pursuing underground economists.

Once organizational actors identify the change agenda as a challenge instead of a chore, there are no limits to learning. Since UIA presented managers with a generic PPA framework, they had to tinker with it to fit it into their units and make it work. A "here's how I'm doing it in my unit" atmosphere emerged, whereby managers learned a great deal from one another's ingenuity.

Make sure that incentives and rewards for transitional work are in place. Since transitions are special times, they may call for special incentives and rewards. At the minimum, implementing the pre-ferred-scenario plan should not be experienced as punitive. Organizational actors are more likely to embark on any given step of a program if there are clear and meaningful incentives. Overly distant goals may not appear rewarding.

EXAMPLE: Admissions, nursing, and pharmacy in a large hospital were all dragging their feet on the new computer-based information-management program. While everyone knew that the new system was inevitable, even overdue, few seemed to be excited about it. The implementation team had focused on the technology and on information flow, not on the impact it would have on the hospital as a social system. Some of the units felt that they would be more exposed. For instance, admissions would know immediately when a bed was available, whereas in the old system nursing had some control over when this information got to admissions. Little had been done to help each unit appreciate how the new system would help them in their work. Even less had been done to help them grapple with its possible punitive effects. *Interdependies*

Reluctant and resistant organizational actors are moved by incentives and work for rewards. If they do not cooperate, they obviously find not cooperating more rewarding (or less punishing) than cooperating. There is a principle here. *Don't* immediately blame organizational players who do not participate in implementation programs. It may well be that they do not see strong enough short-term or even long-term incentives for doing it. *Do* work at helping them find the kinds of intrinsic and extrinsic incentives that will help them stick to programs.

Avoidance mechanisms are potent restraining forces in the implementation of programs. Avoidance will take place if the incentives and rewards for not doing something are stronger than the incentives and rewards for doing it. In your dealings with members of the organization at the implementation stage, it can be a mistake to confuse avoidance with ill will. All of us have a tendency to put off the difficult or distasteful, and we break out of that pattern only under certain conditions. If organizational actors are not implementing some step of a program, if they are putting it off, or if they are implementing it in only a desultory way, use the following check list:

- What punishing consequences are involved with implementing any given step of a program and what is being done to minimize them?
- What rewards are there for not implementing the step and how can these be neutralized?
- Is there a reasonable but firm time line for completing the step?
- Are there rewards for completing the step and are these clear to the those responsible for implementation?
- Do these incentives and rewards fit the needs and wants of those in the target group?

Reshape the implementation program as often as is necessary. *Shaping*, here, refers to rewarding gradual movements toward a desired goal or scenario. The steps leading to a remote goal are sometimes called proximal goals. Research shows that "self-motivation is best summoned and sustained by adopting attainable subgoals that lead to large future ones" (Bandura, 1982, p. 134). In other words, create implementation programs for people instead of trying to slot people into impossible programs.

EXAMPLE: One UIA manager, driven by his own needs to appear hard charging, decided that the PPA system could be installed all at once in his unit. He started with appraisal meetings based on objectives that *would have been set* had there been performance planning sessions the year before (although there had been no such meetings). Then, within a week, he wanted performance planning meetings for the coming year. Too much, too soon in the midst of the turmoil of restructuring. The members of his unit revolted.

CONSEQUENCES AND CONSOLIDATION

The consequences of change projects and the consolidation of changes into the system need special attention.

Consequences

All change projects of any import have both anticipated and unanticipated consequences. Some of the anticipated consequences are intended. Certainly, the preferred scenario outcomes are intended. For instance, when a company installs a just-in-time delivery system with its suppliers, it anticipates and intends that the system will be working by a certain date and that its installation will reduce the parts inventory significantly. Some anticipated consequences, however, are unintended or undesirable. When the managers of a bank decided to downsize and offered a variety of incentives for employees to move to jobs outside the bank, they realized that they would lose some people they would rather keep. They provided incentives to stay for some key workers, but they could not discover a formula that would mean that every person targeted to leave would leave and every person targeted to stay would stay. Since they realized that there would be some anticipated but unintended consequences, they monitored the process very carefully. Unanticipated consequences are another story. If they are desirable, then the company or institution need only to rejoice and make hay while the sun shines! When one airline entered into partnerships with some commuter carriers, they did so in order to channel the commuter passengers to their flights. They did not realize that the lower through-fares would attract more passengers, but that is exactly what happened. All change agents should know that there will probably be some unanticipated undesirable consequences of their change projects and be ready to deal with them. This is especially true of complex change projects.

EXAMPLE: Executives of a department store chain realized that there
would be some dissatisfaction when they broke a lease and closed a
store in a suburban mall near a large midwestern city. But they decided to go ahead anyway, because closing the store was part of a plan
to consolidate and to reset the image of the company. However, they
had in no way anticipated the intensity of the outcry of the community. The owners of the other stores in the mall claimed that, since the
store in question was the anchor store for the mall, closing it would
lead to a domino effect. The members of the community outlined the
ways in which the community would suffer severe economic hardship
because of the closing. The press was filled with articles about social
insensitivity. The store remained open.

It could be argued that the company *should* have anticipated the
hue and cry that took place. The point, however, is that the management of unanticipated and undesirable consequences of a change
project is an integral part of the process. The change model itself—
in terms of current scenario, preferred scenario, and plan of action—
can be used to solve or manage these consequences.

Consolidation

A change of any significance needs to be consolidated, stabilized,
regularized, and internalized. It needs to be allowed to settle into
the guts of the system. Kettner, Daley, and Nichols (1985) state:

In this [consolidation] phase, practitioners try to stabilize identified
strengths and correct weaknesses in the effort. Activities are identified
that will lead to maintenance of the system as planned. Information
and judgments about how the change process succeeded and failed
may provide the basis for future planned change episodes. (p. 31)

In this regard, it is sometimes helpful to review the experience of other
companies and institutions with change projects similar to the one
at hand.

EXAMPLE: Members of the UIA PPA task force discussed the PPA
with other major companies who had recently installed the system or
revamped one already in place. The consensus was that PPA takes a

while to settle into the guts of the system. A great deal of fine-tuning is called for. On the other hand, one company found that its most vigorous opponents became, over time, its most vigorous defenders, wondering how they could have done without it for so long.

Giving a change project time to stabilize is not easy. As to PPA, UIA had to wait out any number of naysayers who tried to sabotage the project in dozens of small ways. But when is patience really patience and not blind persistence? Some projects do fail. At best they are terminated and learned from. Exxon, ignoring the *In Search of Excellence* (Peters & Waterman, 1982) injunction, "stick to your knitting," ventured into the office-technology business—a far cry from oil. When it did not work, they pulled out and probably learned from it. Furthermore, consolidation and stabilization are not the same petrification. As long as environments are turbulent and change is the only constant, a culture of vigilance and the skills needed to manage change must become an integral part of the system.

Appendix A

This appendix is drawn from the seventeen chapters of *Change-Agent Skills A: Assessing and Designing Excellence.*[1] The questions that each of those chapters offers are reprinted here.

FROM CHAPTER 1
INTRODUCTION AND OVERVIEW

The Distinction Between
an Organization and a Business

The following questions will help in distinguishing between the business and the organizational structures that are meant to support the business:

- In what ways do we have a clear idea of what "business" we are in and what our business outcomes are in terms of delivering products and/or services?

- To what extent is it clear to us that our organization—in its structure, processes, and procedures—exists only to support our business?

- In what ways do organizational issues distract us and detract from the delivery of business outcomes?

- How effective are we in linking changes in organizational structure, processes, and procedures to improvement in the delivery of business outcomes?

---

[1]From *Change-Agent Skills A: Assessing and Designing Excellence* by G. Egan, 1988, San Diego, CA: University Associates. Copyright 1988 by University Associates. Reprinted by permission.

Excellence

The following questions can provide some initial focus on what your company, agency, institution, or unit needs to do to pursue excellence:

- How excellent is our company or institution?
- To what degree are the basics outlined in this chapter in place in our system?
- What package do we need to develop to become an exemplar in our field?
- What is our formula?

FROM CHAPTER 2
MARKETS, CLIENTS, CUSTOMERS

**Assessing the Needs and Wants
of Customers in Markets of Choice**

Units with internal customers should find answers to the following questions:

- Who are the people who receive my work?
- What do they need from me?
- How can I give them what is needed?

The following questions are designed to help you assess the wants and needs of both internal and external customers and clients.

- How well do we do our market research with respect to external markets? with respect to internal markets?
- How well do we understand our external markets? our internal markets?
- How well do we understand our clients and customers in these markets?
- How thoroughly are the needs and wants of customers in these markets identified?
- How well do we use the information that comes from formal and informal customer-needs assessments? What differences do the data make?
- How clearly are customers or clients and their needs distinguished from the needs and wants of other stakeholders, such as stockholders, managers, and directors?

FROM CHAPTER 3
MANAGING THE BUSINESS ENVIRONMENT

The following questions can help a system determine how excellent it is in terms of understanding and managing the environment.

- How proactive (as opposed to reactive) are we toward the environment?
- How well do we monitor the environmental trends that affect the way we do business?
- What individuals, systems, or trends are important or critical? In what ways?
- What environmental threats do we currently face?
- How well are we managing these threats?
- What unexploited opportunities have we identified in the environment?
- How well are we developing them?
- How time-sensitive are these externalities? How quickly do we have to act if we are to take advantage of a significant opportunity or fend off a significant threat?
- What environmental events or crises have taken us by surprise?
- What scanning procedures do we need to put in place when the environment is especially turbulent?
- To what degree do our findings about the environment affect our strategic direction?

FROM CHAPTER 4
MISSION AND BUSINESS VALUES

**The Mission and
the Mission Statement**

The following questions, which relate to both a company or institution and its subunits, will help in developing appropriate mission statements and refining them.

- To what degree have we developed a realistic and forceful mission statement?

- How closely is this mission statement related to our markets and the needs and wants of customers within these markets?
- To what degree has this mission statement been communicated in practical ways to everyone in the system?
- To what degree is our mission statement a driving force for those working here?
- If there are conflicts over our mission, how are these conflicts managed?
- Do subunits have their own mission statements?
- To what degree are the mission statements of subunits integrated with our business mission?

Business Values and Policies

The following questions can help a system focus on its business philosophy:

- To what degree do we have a coherent business philosophy, that is, a set of major beliefs, values, and policies, which permeate and guide our work?
- How clear is this philosophy to all who work here?
- How clearly has our philosophy been communicated to our clients or customers?
- To what degree is the way we operate consistent with our espoused philosophy?

A People Mission

The following questions will help in the search for excellence in the management of human resources:

- Do we have a coherent people mission?
- To what degree is this major statement concerning the quality of life of our employees integrated with our business mission?
- To what degree does this statement drive the behavior of the organization?
- To what degree have QWL policies been designed into our organization rather than added on?

- To what degree have subunits in the organization derived explicit people missions from the overall people mission of the company or institution?

FROM CHAPTER 5
ESTABLISHING MAJOR CATEGORIES
OF PRODUCTS AND SERVICES

The following questions about principle agendas will help in determining major categories of products and services:

- What are the major areas in which we can deliver quality products and services?
- How do these categories relate to our overall mission?
- To what degree are these categories based on market research?
- Which categories should be dropped? Which should be added?
- What evidence do we have that we are sticking to our knitting?
- How effective have we been in carving out a niche in which we are known and respected for our quality products or services?

FROM CHAPTER 6
STRATEGY

Strategic Planning

A strategic plan, at least in its basic form, deals with the following factors: the business mission, the major categories of products or services the business intends to provide, the markets and customers that constitute the targets of these products or services, the notion of market niche, the internal resources of the company or institution, and the relevant opportunities and threats posed by the environment. The answers to questions about each of these factors constitute the criteria for determining the business game plan. The following questions provide examples:

- In what ways does our mission need to be updated?
- In light of our mission, what major categories of products or services do we want to provide?
- Do we have what it takes to develop markets?
- How ready are existing markets to receive our products or services?
- Given current competition, can we carve a niche for ourselves in the marketplace?
- To what degree do we have the resources such as expertise and financing to manufacture and/or distribute these products or deliver these services?
- To be successful, what environmental opportunities do we need to take advantage of?
- To avoid failure, what environmental threats need to be managed?
- What degree of risk is involved in all of this and to what degree are we prepared to take risks?

The following questions will help you analyze the current state of strategic planning in your company or institution:

- How well does our planning stimulate creativity and foster productivity-centered communication?
- How skilled are our people in thinking strategically? That is, do they think about creating the future rather than waiting for it to happen?
- To what degree is strategic thinking blotted out by our day-to-day operations?
- What kind of strategic plan do we have?
- How well does our strategic plan integrate (a) market/client needs, major environmental factors, and our mission with (b) our business philosophy and values and (c) our choice of major categories of products and services?
- How often do we review and update our strategic plan?
- How well do we drive the strategy down into the guts of our company or institution?
- To what degree is there is a sense of strategic direction in our company or institution?

FROM CHAPTER 7
PRODUCTS AND SERVICES

Renewed Focus on Quality

The following questions can be used as a check list in assessing the delivery of products or services:

- Is it clear to everyone in the organization that products and services that satisfy customer needs constitute the heart of our business?
- Do our products and services meet our clients' needs and wants? Are they valued by our customers?
- What do our products and services offer that makes them different from and better than those of our competitors?
- Do we deliver high-quality products and services? How do we know?
- Do we have a quality-assurance plan or program?
- Do we deliver our products and services in a timely fashion?
- Do we try to compete on quality rather than price?
- To what degree do we continually try to upgrade our products and services?

Internal Customers

The following questions may help you assess the quality of customer service in your system:

- Do we have a realistic and viable customer-service strategy?
- To what extent does this strategy include both external and internal customers?
- Do we have customer-oriented front-line people?
- How customer-friendly are our internal systems, that is, our physical facilities, policies, procedures, methods, and communication processes?
- To what degree are customers or clients systematically asked for feedback?
- How effective is the response to this feedback?

- What do our customers think of our dealings with them?
- How easy is it for customers and clients to make their concerns known to the people in the organization who can manage these concerns?
- How responsive is the organization to customer or client needs, wants, and concerns?
- What kind of priority do good customer and client relationships have with us?
- To what degree are fresh approaches to client relationships developed and implemented?

FROM CHAPTER 8
WORK PROGRAMS

The following questions will help assess work programs and quality-of-life considerations:

- How clear are the desired accomplishments (products or service outcomes) toward which the work program is directed? How well do we know what we are doing?
- To what degree is there a clear, step-by-step work program for every outcome?
- Have we made sure that each work program is as simple and as cost effective as possible? If so, how?
- In the case of complex work programs, how clearly and effectively are subprograms integrated with one another?
- To what degree has the efficiency of complex work programs been determined by some systematic programing methodology, such as PERT?
- To what degree have QWL considerations been designed into the work programs?
- How well do the work programs provide variety, a sense of completeness, and meaning?
- To what degree can workers give themselves ongoing feedback on their performance?
- How well do we build a strategic perspective into work-program decisions?

FROM CHAPTER 9
MANAGING MATERIAL RESOURCES

The following questions can be used in the search for excellence in the management of material resources.

The Management of Financial Resources

- How well are our finances managed?
- To what degree are realistic budgets established and followed?
- How is our budget flexibility related to the changing business needs?
- What kinds of financial problems do we face?
- How effectively are these problems being managed?

The Management of Material Resources

- Do we have access to the material resources we need to get our work done?
- How are we assuring that material resources will be available as needed?
- How well are logistics problems handled?
- Do we have the tools we need to get our work done efficiently and effectively?
- What are our relationships with our suppliers like?
- Are cost-effective programs, such as just-in-time delivery, in place?
- In what kind of repair is our equipment?
- Are preventive maintenance programs in place?
- Is new technology (for manufacturing products or delivering services) periodically reviewed?
- Is cost-effective new technology adopted to make the delivery of programs more effective and efficient?

FROM CHAPTER 10
UNIT PERFORMANCE PLANNING

The following questions can help in assessing the status of the current unit performance plan:

- To what degree does each unit in our organization have a realistic performance plan?

- How well does this plan translate the overall strategic plan of the company or institution into operational realities?

- How well does this plan integrate the unit with other units for which it is either an internal supplier or customer?

- To what degree does the unit performance plan actually help integrate work programs and drive behavior in the unit?

- To what degree do the people who work in this unit understand the unit's current strategic priorities?

- Are the objectives of the unit performance plan clear enough to help individuals to establish realistic individual performance plans?

- If there is no unit performance plan, how are unit priorities set?

FROM CHAPTER 11
THE DIVISION OF LABOR

Structure: Establishing Subunits

The following are questions that can help in assessing the ways in which work has been divided among the units of the company or institution:

- Do we have our structure right? That is, does it enable us to deliver business outcomes efficiently and effectively?

- Which work units in our organization are not really pulling their weight? How much fat is there in the system?

- Could we eliminate or combine any units and still operate quite well?

- How often do we examine and revise our structure to keep up with changes in our business?

- What kind of structure do successful companies or institutions in our business have?

- When we have changed our structure, have the changes led to better business outcomes?
- To what degree have we fallen into the trap of reorganizing when the real problem was that we did not have our business right?

Roles: Getting People
To Do the Right Things

Following are some questions that can be asked to determine whether the division of labor within the organizational unit is contributing to excellence in the delivery of products and services to customers:

- Are all the positions we have in the unit needed, that is, do they actually contribute to business outcomes?
- Which activities now carried out in the unit would, if dropped, make little or no difference? In other words, where is the fat in the unit?
- How do job descriptions indicate the kinds of outcomes or accomplishments expected of the person who holds the position?
- How clear and realistic are these accomplishment-oriented job descriptions?
- To what degree are job descriptions revised as the work changes?
- To what extent do we add or drop positions as the work changes?
- How clear are the person specifications for each job?
- How flexible are the roles? How easily adapted to changing conditions?
- In what ways can the roles in the unit be made more meaningful?
- What do we do upfront to avoid role ambiguity? conflict? overload?

FROM CHAPTER 12
COMPETENT UNITS WITH COMPETENT PEOPLE

Competent Units

Below are some questions that can be asked to determine the competency of the organizational units in a company or institution:

- How well specified is the mission of our unit?

- How well is the mission of our unit integrated with the mission of our parent unit and the overall mission of the company or institution?
- How well is the mission of our unit communicated to those who work in it?
- To what degree does the mission of our unit actually drive the behavior of those who work here?
- How well does our unit know our internal and external customers and their needs?
- How well do we deal with our internal and external customers?
- What kind of reputation do our products or services have?
- What do our customers say of us?
- What kind of spirit exists in our unit?
- What would we need to do to become an exemplary unit in the organization?

The Development of Human Resources

Companies and institutions with successful enculturation programs come up with creative answers to the following questions:

- What are the needs of the system with respect to the newcomer?
- What are the needs of the newcomer with respect to the system?
- What outcomes or accomplishments related to both productivity and quality of work life constitute initial integration?
- What programs can be developed that will help ensure that newcomers become both productive and at home as quickly as possible?

Here are some questions than can help an organization or a unit focus on the management of human resources:

- What kind of organizational human-resources strategy do we have?
- How well is that strategy communicated to and implemented in each organizational unit?
- How well do we recruit people for this unit?
- To what degree do we get people who are competent? eager? compatible with the mission of the unit? with the teams in the unit?
- How well do we enculturate or socialize people into the unit?

- To what degree do we have the right people for the right jobs?
- What do we do with our problem people?
- What do we do with people who have peaked and are growing restless?
- How well do we manage our star performers?
- How well are managers and supervisors equipped with the kinds of coaching and counseling skills needed to help problem performers?
- What problems do we have, such as turnover, that indicate that we have staffing problems?
- How well do we develop our workers through training or other experiences?
- What are we doing with workers whose skills are outdated?
- What do we do with productive but "difficult" people?
- What is our current career-development strategy?

FROM CHAPTER 13
TEAMWORK: THE REINTEGRATION
OF LABOR

Interunit Teamwork

The following are some questions that can be asked about the quality of interunit teamwork:

- How well do different units work with one another to increase productivity?
- What "empires" have we let develop?
- What significant partnerships have been established with key units and what further partnerships need to be developed?
- To what degree does interunit competition, jealousy, or politics interfere with productivity?
- To what degree does interunit behavior actually decrease productivity?
- In what ways does a spirit of interunit teamwork permeate the organization?

- What innovative forms of collaboration can be developed between functions?

Principles of Effective Teamwork

The following are some questions that can be asked about teamwork within each unit of a company or institution:

- To what degree does a spirit of teamwork permeate our unit?
- How well can each member of the unit answer this question: In what ways can I cooperate/collaborate with other individuals or other units in order to get the work of the unit done?
- In what ways do we underuse teamwork in getting our work done?
- In what ways do we overuse teamwork at the expense of efficiency and effectiveness?
- When people do work in teams, how well is their work coordinated?
- In what ways does our teamwork enhance business outcomes?
- What do we do about nonteam players?
- What do we do about players who are overly dependent on the team?
- What kind of balance is there between teamwork and individual effort?
- To what degree do we use quality circles or some other form of intra-unit collaborative problem solving and innovation development?

FROM CHAPTER 14
COMMUNICATION PROCESSES

Conflict Management

A conflict can be said to be resolved when the parties in question are fully satisfied with an outcome. This means that there is either no residual frustration or at least not enough to precipitate future episodes. However, conflict, like most human problems, is not solved or resolved, but managed. The fact that today's frustration is managed more or less is no guarantee that tomorrow will not spawn its own. When two parties emerge from a conflict, the bottom-line questions deal with productivity and quality of life:

- Did they come up with a decision that they both can live with, at least for now?
- Does this decision in some way favor, or at least not stand in the way of, the productivity of the system?
- Is the relationship between the two parties still intact and workable?
- Does the decision help improve, or at least not stand in the way of, the quality of life of other members?
- Does the quality of the decision merit its financial and psychological costs? If not, what has been learned that can contribute to making conflict management in this system more cost effective in the future?
- Has this conflict situation helped the parties reflect on and clarify personal values, system values, and the interaction between the two?

Interunit Communication

Here are some questions about interunit communication:

- To what degree do we establish terms of reference for our interactions with other relevant organizational units?
- How well does this unit share information needed for productivity with other units in the organization?
- To what degree do we get the information we need from other units?
- To what degree do we give feedback to and get feedback from other units with respect to products or services in order to increase productivity?
- In what ways do we engage constructively with other units in the appraisal of one another's performance?
- How well do we engage in collaborative problem solving with other units?
- To what degree do we have innovation-focused dialogs with other units?
- How effectively do we work through conflicts with other units in the system?

Interpersonal Communication

The following questions relate to interpersonal communication within a unit:

- How well do we see one another in this unit as internal customers?
- How effectively do we share information with one another in this unit?
- How open are we to giving feedback to and receiving feedback from one another?
- How realistic are our appraisals of one another in this unit?
- What is the quality of collaborative problem solving in this unit?
- To what degree do we engage in innovation dialogs in this unit?
- How effectively do we handle conflicts with one another in this unit?

FROM CHAPTER 15
THE REWARD SYSTEM:
KEEPING MOTIVATION HIGH

Here are some questions about incentives and rewards:

- To what degree is getting the work of the system done the primary reward in this system?
- To what degree are there incentives in all units to accomplish goals?
- What kind of disincentives interfere with our work?
- To what degree are incentives followed by meaningful rewards? What promises are made but not kept?
- To what extent do we have the right mix of incentives and rewards for our work force?
- How effectively do individuals establish meaningful reward systems for themselves?
- To what degree is the system managed so as to avoid punishment?
- To what degree is there a "culture of avoidance" in the system?
- How are avoiders treated?

FROM CHAPTER 16
INDIVIDUAL PERFORMANCE PLANS

Here are some questions that can be asked about the status of individual performance planning in any organization:

- To what degree are effective performance planning practices in place?
- To what degree are individual performance plans linked to ongoing feedback and realistic appraisal?
- How collaborative (with managers) is the setting of performance objectives?
- How well do individuals know the priorities of the unit performance plan?
- To what degree is individual performance planning merely *pro forma*? To what degree does it actually drive behavior?
- To what degree are individual plans updated as unit priorities change?
- What might be done to make individual performance planning more effective?

FROM CHAPTER 17
EFFECTIVE MANAGEMENT AND LEADERSHIP

Executive/Executive-Team Leadership

The following are some questions that can be asked about executive leadership in any company or institution:

- To what degree is our chief executive a person of vision?
- What kind of vision and creativity is found among the chief executive's top team?
- How creative are the agendas established by the top person or team?
- How well are these agendas communicated to the rest of the organization?
- How enthusiastically do people in the organization rally around these agendas?
- To what degree does the top team establish a ferment of learning and problem solving around the principal agendas of the company or institution?
- How well does the top team support these agendas through incentives and rewards?
- How rewarding is it to help carry out these agendas?

- To what extent do top team members persist in promoting their agendas? How effective are they in follow through?
- To what degree do the members of the organization see these agendas through to completion?

Managerial Leadership

The following are key questions in determining the leadership of a manager:

- In what ways does this manager express managerial vision? establish creative agendas? motivate subordinates? establish a climate of learning and problem solving in the unit? persist in getting things done?
- To what degree does this manager make sure that the mission of the next higher unit and of the company or institution is communicated to the troops?
- How well does this manager see himself or herself as a manager of productivity-related innovation and change?
- What productivity and QWL innovations has this manager instituted?
- How creatively does this manager go about ordinary managerial tasks? planning creatively? organizing creatively? coordinating creatively? facilitating creatively? instituting creative control systems?
- How effectively does this manager establish productivity-related incentives and rewards in the unit?
- How effectively does this manager collaborate with subordinates in setting performance objectives?
- How effectively has this manager established a "culture of feedback" in his or her unit?
- How effectively does this manager use coaching or counseling as a way of adding value to the work done by people in his or her unit?
- How well does this manager protect his or her subordinates from internal and external threats?
- How effective a mentor is this manager?
- How creatively does this manager interact with managers of other units?
- How creatively does this manager do the hard things in his or her unit, such as giving hard messages, letting people go, and cutting costs?

- How creatively does this manager manage the financial and material resources of the unit?
- How creatively does this manager manage his or her subordinate managers?
- How well does this manager manage his or her relationship with the boss?
- What does this manager need to do to become an exemplary manager? To what degree is this possible?

Supervisory Leadership

Since some supervisors are mini-managers, some of the questions under managerial leadership might be relevant. For others, the following questions might suffice:

- In what ways does this supervisor express vision? establish creative agendas? motivate operators in his or her unit? get operators to learn and solve problems?
- How aware is this supervisor of the mission of this unit? of the company or institution?
- How much of a "sense of people" does this supervisor have?
- How effective are his or her people skills?
- What supervisory innovations has this supervisor introduced?
- What does this supervisor need to do to become an exemplary supervisor? To what degree is this possible?
- In what ways have operators grown under his or her supervision?
- To what degree are supervisors encouraged to innovate?

Professional/Technical Leadership

The following questions are relevant for professional or technical leaders:

- How well does this professional stay abreast of the developments in his or her field?
- In what ways has he or she contributed to the field?
- How effectively does this professional adapt what is new in the field to the needs of this company or institution?

- What kind of model for others is this professional?
- How effectively does this professional teach/train others in the organization?

Operator Leadership

The following questions are relevant for operators in any organization:

- Who are the exemplary operators in this organization and what makes them stand apart?
- To what degree are operators given incentives to find more effective ways of doing their work?
- What kinds of ideas do operators offer?
- What could be done to help operators become more creative?
- How do operators experience the "geometry" of the organization? In what ways do they see themselves on the cutting edge rather than on the bottom?
- What kind of attention and respect do operators in this organization receive?

Appendix B

OD READINESS CHECK LIST

The instrument on the following page summarizes the chief indicators of OD readiness and assigns each indicator a weight according to its relative degree of criticalness. The following interpretations of scoring can be helpful to consultants: a score of less than 50 would suggest training, small-scale projects, and crisis interventions; 50-70 would indicate management development and pre-OD activities; 70 and higher would indicate that the consultant test the willingness of the organization to commit itself to planned change.

OD READINESS CHECK LIST[1]

Instructions: Using the following check list, indicate the degree to which each of the fifteen dimensions is a concern to you with regard to the organization's readiness for OD. Circle the number under the appropriate heading for each factor. Each dimension has been scaled according to its relative importance in predicting the organization's receptivity to OD interventions. Total the scores for an overall OD readiness index.

General Considerations	No Concern	Mild Concern	Moderate Concern	Significant Concern	Critical Concern
1. Size	4	3	2	1	0
2. Growth Rate	4	3	2	1	0
3. Crisis (potential positive or negative influence)	4	3	2	1	0
4. Macroeconomics	4	3	2	1	0
5. OD History	4	3	2	1	0
6. Culture	4	3	2	1	0
Resources					
7. Time Commitment	8	6	4	2	0
8. Money	8	6	4	2	0
9. Access to People	8	6	4	2	0
10. Labor Contract Limitations	8	6	4	2	0
11. Structural Flexibility	8	6	4	2	0
People Variables					
12. Interpersonal Skills	12	9	6	3	0
13. Management Development	12	9	6	3	0
14. Flexibility at the Top	12	9	6	3	0
15. Internal Change Agents	12	9	6	3	0

Total Readiness Score   _____

---

[1]From "OD Readiness" by J.W. Pfeiffer and J.E. Jones, 1978, in *The Cutting Edge*, edited by W.W. Burke. San Diego, CA: University Associates. Reprinted by permission.

References

Albrecht, K., & Zemke, R. (1985). *Service America: Doing business in the new Economy.* Homewood, IL: Dow Jones-Irwin.

Argyris, C. (1982). *Reasoning, learning, and action: Individual and organizational.* San Francisco: Jossey-Bass.

Bandura, A. (1982). Self-efficacy mechanism in human agency. *American Psychologist, 37,* 122-147.

Beckhard, R. (1985). *Managing change in organizations: Participant's workbook.* Reading, MA: Addison-Wesley.

Beckhard, R., and Harris, R. T. (1987). *Organizational transitions: Managing complex change.* Reading, MA: Addison-Wesley.

Bennis, W., & Nanus, B. (1985). *Leaders: The strategies for taking charge.* New York: Harper & Row.

Bernstein, A. (1986, March 31). Chopping health care costs: Labor picks up the ax. *Business Week,* pp. 78-80.

Blake, R., & Mouton, J. S. (1982). *Productivity: The human side.* New York: AMACOM.

Cohen, M. D., March, J. G., & Olsen, J. P. (1972). A garbage-can model of organizational choice. *Administrative Sciences Quarterly, 17,* 1-25.

Cole, H. P., and Sarnoff, D. (1980). Creativity and counseling. *Personnel and Guidance Journal, 59,* 140-146.

Cook, J. (1987, February 23). There are no garage sales here. *Forbes,* p. 75.

D'Zurilla, T. J., & Nezu, A. (1980). A study of the generation-of-alternatives process in social problem solving. *Cognitive Therapy and Research, 4,* 67-72.

Egan, G. (1985). *Change agent skills in helping and human service settings.* Monterey, CA: Brooks/Cole.

Egan, G. (1986). *The skilled helper: A systematic approach to effective helping.* Monterey, CA: Brooks/Cole.

Egan, G. (1988). *Change-agent skills A: Assessing and Designing Excellence.* San Diego, CA: University Associates.

Einhorn, H. J., & Hogarth, R. M. (1987, January-February). Decision making: Going forward in reverse. *Harvard Business Review*, pp. 66.

Feingold, S.N. (1984). Merging careers: Occupations for post-industrial society. *The Futurist, 18*(1), 9-16.

Ferguson, M. (1980). *The aquarian conspiracy: Personal and social transformation in the 1980s.* Los Angeles: J. P. Tarcher.

Fink, S. (1986). *Crisis management: Planning for the inevitable.* New York: AMACOM.

Fix, J. L. (1986, March 10). Disappointed but insured. *Forbes*, pp. 56, 58.

Forbes, M. S., Jr. (1986, March 10). People are the answer. *Forbes.*

Gelatt, H. B., Varenhorst, B., & Carey, R. (1972). *Deciding: A leader's guide.* Princeton, NJ: College Entrance Examination Board.

Geneen, H. S., with Moscow, A. (1984). *Managing.* New York: Doubleday.

Godwin, G. (1985). *The finishing school.* New York: Viking Penguin.

Goleman, D. (1985). *Vital lies, simple truths: The psychology of self-deception.* New York: Simon & Schuster.

Goslin, D. A. (1985). Decision making and the social fabric. *Society, 22*(2), 7-11.

Gottfredson, G. D. (1984). A theory-ridden approach to program evaluation. *American Psychologist, 39,* 278-287.

Hadley, A. T. (1986). *The straw giant.* New York: Random House.

Heppner, P. (1978). A review of problem-solving literature and its relationship to the counseling process. *Journal of Counseling Psychology, 25,* 366-375.

Hickman, C. R., & Silva, M. A. (1984). *Creating excellence.* New York: New American Library.

Hornstein, H. A. (1986). *Managerial courage: Revitalizing your company without sacrificing your job.* New York: John Wiley.

How benefits can backfire. (1986, April 7). *Forbes*, p. 8.

Janis, I. L., & Mann, L. (1977). *Decision making: A psychological analysis of conflict, choice, and commitment.* New York: Free Press.

John Psarouthakis: Whipping underdog companies into shape. (1986, August 11). *Business Week*, p. 74.

Kanter, R. M. (1983). *Change masters: Innovation for productivity in the American corporation.* New York: Simon & Schuster.

Kettner, P., Daley, J. M., & Nichols, A. W. (1985). *Initiating change in organizations and communities.* Monterey, CA: Brooks/Cole.

Kirkpatrick, D. L. (1985). *How to manage change effectively.* San Francisco: Jossey-Bass.

Leonard, B. (1986, December 1). Make mine private. *Forbes*, pp. 56-57.

Lewin, K. (1969). Quasi-stationary social equilibria and the problem of permanent change. In W. G. Bennis, K. D. Benne, & R. Chin (Eds.), *The planning of change*. New York: Holt, Rinehart, & Winston.

Locke, E. A., & Latham, G. P. (1984). *Goal setting: A motivational technique that works*. Englewood Cliffs, NJ: Prentice-Hall.

Los Angeles County Public Administrator. (1986). Producing more for less. *Administrative Management*, 47(3), 30.

Machan, D. (1987, February 9). Pink-slip time. *Forbes*, pp. 118, 120.

March, J. G. (1982). Theories of choice and making decisions. Society, 19, 29-39.

Marcom, J., Jr. (1987, January 14). British industry suffers from failure to heed basics of marketing. *The Wall Street Journal*, p. 1.

Merwin, J. (1987, January 26). The little drug company that could. *Forbes*.

Moreas, G. (1985). *Un flic de l'interieur*. Paris: Edition 1.

Murray, A. E. (1986, March 17). How to catch tax cheaters. *Fortune*, pp. 124-125.

Naisbitt, J., & Aburdene, P. (1985). *Re-inventing the corporation: Transforming your job and your company for the new information society*. New York: Warner Books.

Nasar, S. (1986, March 17). Jobs go begging at the bottom. *Fortune*, pp. 33-35.

Nayak, P. R., & Ketteringham, J. M. (1986). *Breakthroughs*. New York: Rawson Associates.

Peters, T. J., & Waterman, R. W., Jr. (1982). *In search of excellence*. New York: Harper & Row.

Pittel, L. (1986, March 24). Too little, too late. *Forbes*.

Pfeiffer, J. W., & Jones, J. E. (1978). OD readiness. In W. E. Burke (Ed.), *The cutting edge: Current theory and practice in organization development*. San Diego, CA: University Associates.

Pinchot, G. P., III. (1985). *Intrapreneuring*. New York: Harper & Row.

Raab, A. A. (1985). Major changes in a traditional manufacturing facility. *Organization Development Journal*, 3(2), 27-29.

Robertshaw, J. E., Mecca, S. J., & Rerick, M. N. (1978). *Problem-solving: A systems approach*. New York: Petrocelli Books.

Rowan, R. (1986). *The intuitive manager*. Boston, MA: Little, Brown.

Spier, M. S. (1973). Kurt Lewin's "force-field analysis." In J. E. Jones & J. W. Pfeiffer (Eds.), *The 1973 annual handbook for group facilitators*. San Diego, CA: University Associates.

Spragins, E. E. (1986, March 3). For Foote Cone, the answer is still "whole-brain" thinking. *Business Week*.

Stein, B. A. (1980). Quality of work life in context: What every practitioner should know. Unpublished manuscript. Cambridge, MA: Goodmeasure.

Stein, B. A., & Kanter, R. M. (1980). Building the parallel organization: Creating mechanisms for permanent quality of work life. *Journal of Applied Behavioral Science, 16,* 371-385.

The vanishing vacation. (1986, February 9). *Forbes,* p. 13.

Walden, B. (1986, December 21). Success—it's up for grabs. *New York Times,* p. 12.

Weick, K. E. (1969). *The social psychology of organizing.* Reading, MA: Addison-Wesley.

Weick, K. E. (1979). *The social psychology of organizing* (3rd ed.). Reading, MA: Addison-Wesley.

Whimbey, A., & Lochhead, J. (1986). *Problem solving and comprehension.* Hillsdale, NJ: Erlbaum.

Wriston, W. (1986). *Risk and other four-letter words.* New York: Harper & Row.

Name Index

Subject Index